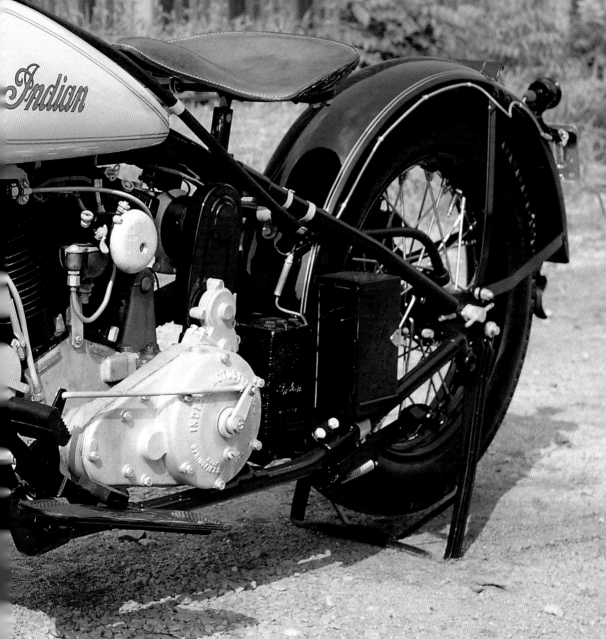

· MOTORCYCLE COLOR HISTORY ·

INDIAN CHIEF
Motorcycles *1922–1953*

Jerry Hatfield

Motorbooks International
Publishers & Wholesalers

First published in 1997 by Motorbooks
International Publishers & Wholesalers, 729
Prospect Avenue, PO Box 1, Osceola, WI
54020-0001 USA

Motorbooks International is a certified trademark,
registered with the United States Patent Office

The information in this book is true and complete
to the best of our knowledge. All recommendations
are made without any guarantee on the part of the
author or Publisher, who also disclaim any liability
incurred in connection with the use of this data or
specific details

We recognize that some words, model names and
designations, for example, mentioned herein are the
property of the trademark holder. We use them for
identification purposes only. This is not an official
publication

Motorbooks International books are also available
at discounts in bulk quantity for industrial or sales-
promotional use. For details write to Special Sales
Manager at the Publisher's address

Library of Congress Cataloging-in-Publication Data
Hatfield, Jerry H.
    Indian Chief motorcycles, 1922–1953/Jerry Hatfield
      p. cm.--(Motorcycle color history)
    Includes index.
    ISBN 0-7603-0332-0 (pbk.)
    1. Indian motorcycle--History. I. Title. II. Series:
Motorbooks International motorcycle color history.
TL448.I5H36   1997
629.227'5--dc21   97-26987

On the front cover: An original machine is a great rarity
among motorcycles as collectible as Indian Chiefs.
Rick La Plante's 1938 Chief wears the patina so loved
by true devotees of the marque.

On the frontispiece: Rider's-eye view of the 1948 Chief
instrument panel. Red light is for the generator. *Jeff
Hackett*

On the title page: Chiefs received a decidedly Scout-like
look when they were updated for 1932. A taller front
end and new gas tanks made for a sleek profile.
Dennis Craig owns this handsome example.

On the back cover: Top: The proud Chief line came to
an end in 1953. Despite strong rider and dealer
loyalty, the challenging postwar market, a rising flood
of less expensive offerings from England, and Indian's
disastrous lightweight program ultimately led to the
company's demise. Bottom: This beautifully restored
1946 Chief belongs to John Dufilie. *Jeff Hackett*

Printed in Hong Kong

Contents

	Acknowledgments	6
Chapter 1	**Many Indians but No Chiefs** *1901–1920*	8
Chapter 2	**Chiefs of the Roaring Twenties** *1921–1929*	14
Chapter 3	**Bottoming Out and Climbing Back** *1930–1934*	28
Chapter 4	**Better Roads Mean Faster Riding** *1935–1936*	42
Chapter 5	**Mixed Results** *1937–1939*	60
Chapter 6	**Looks to Kill For** *1940–1942*	76
Chapter 7	**Drafted** *1942–1945*	90
Chapter 8	**Last of the Wigwam Chiefs** *1946–1948*	96
Chapter 9	**The Twilight Years** *1949–1953*	108
Chapter 10	**Indian Fun**	118
Appendix	**Colors and Other Finishing Details**	124
	Index	128

Acknowledgments

First, a big thank you to the good friends who've helped me with this and other books: Butch Baer, the late Earl Bentley, Pete Bollenbach of Bollenbach Engineering, Stan Brock, Max and Suzi Bubeck, Woody Carson, Jim Dennie, Don Doody, the late Clyde Earl, Bob Finn, Tom Gadd, Jerry Greer of Jerry Greer's Indian Engineering, Jeff Grigsby of Indian Motorworks, Jeff Hackett, Hans Halberstadt, Dave Halliday, Harley-Davidson Motor Company, Gene Harper, the late Jimmy and Florence Hill, the late Ed Kretz Sr. and Mary Kretz, Elmer Lower, Don and Carolyn Miller, the late Emmett Moore, Bruce Palmer, John Parker, Gary Phelps, John Rank, Dr. Martin Jack Rosenblum of Harley-Davidson, Bob and Shorty Stark of Starklite Cycle, Jim Sutter of Indian Motercycle Supply Inc., Doug Van Allen, Toney Watson, and George and Mili Yarocki.

The Bubecks, Jeff Grigsby, the Millers, the Starks, and the Yarockies hosted this "starving artist" for a night or more.

Next, an equally heartfelt thank you to the first-time contributors and hosts who helped so much in completing this book: Peter Arundel, Glenn and Denny Bator, Allan Carter, Chuck and Stephanie Myles, and Walt and Lucile Timme.

Thanks also to other first-time helpers: Steve Baird; Jim Bowker; Rich Carrano; Allan Carter; Susie Christian; Jim, Debbie, and Scout Christian; John Corrick; Dennis Craig; Tim Cunningham; Paul D'Amico; Robert "Deke" Diegal; Jim and Susan Dingess; Mark Dooley; William H. "Doug" Douglas; John Dufile; Mike and Debbie Fisher; Shirley Hansen; Rick La Plante; Tony Milen; Mike and Vicki Milton; Shantell Morgan; Barbara Ann Moss; Erling and Daniel Olberg; John O'Neal; Deano Paul of HP Indian Cycle; Wilson Plank of American Indian Specialists; Doug Strange; Mike Steckley of Vintage Motorcycles; Vic Sucher; Kent Thompson; Ted Tine and Essex Motorsports; Bub Tramontin; Dan Vine; Doug Wanke; Michael Karl Witzel; Tom Woertink; and Mort Wood.

I'm indebted to the Research Center, Henry Ford Museum and Greenfield Village for the use of the E. Paul du Pont Papers. All du Pont correspondence and documents of the Indian Motocycle Company in this book are cited to "E. Paul du Pont Papers, Research Center, Henry Ford Museum and Greenfield Village."

Thanks to the following for their special contributions: Butch Baer, the late Earl Bentley, Bob Finn, the late Jimmy and Florence Hill, and the late Emmett Moore, who were the sources of Indian archival photos. George and Mili Yarocki, through their literature collection, were the source of much Indian documentation not otherwise available. Allan Carter's reminiscences were unique.

–Jerry Hatfield

Chapter 1

Many Indians but No Chiefs
1901–1920

At the turn of the century, bicycles were the craze, and pedalers were all about either having a good time or huffing and puffing to their jobs in the cities. Horses were still the choice of many gentlemen of commerce. Trains handled all long-distance overland travel, and within Chicago, New York, and a few other cities, trains also offered city dwellers a cheap ride to work.

Into this environment came the first commercially available automobiles. They hardly made a dent. Cars were so expensive that their owners were mainly bankers, doctors, lawyers, and other professionals. Motorized traffic remained an oddity confined to cities with paved streets, save for an occasional 10- or 15-mile cross-country venture that at completion marked the driver as the hit of the cocktail circuit. Cross-country drivers had a right to brag, for cities were linked by dirt ruts that were accurately described as trails, even into the 1920s.

In 1901, with affordable automobiles nowhere in sight, founders George Hendee and Oscar Hedstrom had a right to feel the future was unlimited for their newly launched Indian motocycles—they spelled the name without the "r." Quickly, the Hendee Manufacturing Company of Springfield, Massachusetts, became the world's largest motorcycle manufacturer. Indian's success was largely due to three design factors: bicycle styling that didn't scare away prospects, performance that was

Out for a cruise on a 1904 single is cofounder George Hendee. The diamond (bicycle) framed singles promised the ease and safety of the pedal bike without physical exertion. The single-speed 98-pound "motocycle" (Indian's term) would run from 5 to 35 miles per hour. Produced from 1901 through 1909, this design from cofounder Oscar Hedstrom gave Indian an annual growth rate of 50 percent per year. Indian archival photo via Bob Finn (hereafter, "Indian/Finn")

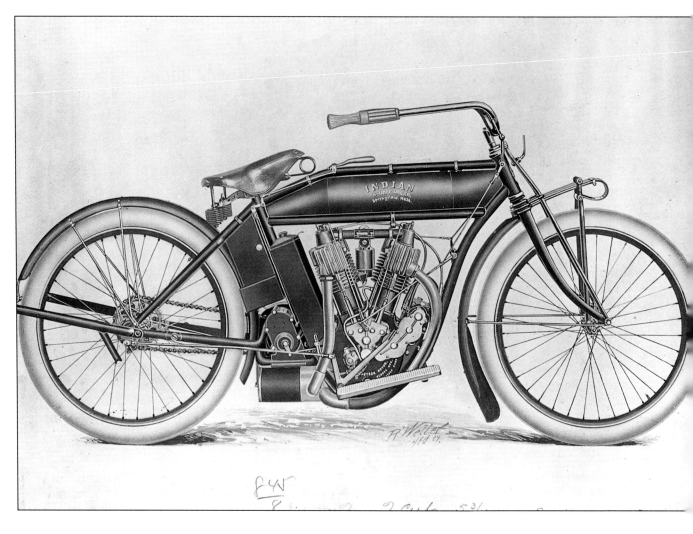

This 1911 two-speed 61.92-cubic-inch (1,014-cc) twin was similar to the models that finished 1-2-3 in the famous 1911 Isle of Man Tourist Trophy race. The F-head engine layout was standard for the era and features overhead inlet valves and side-mounted, inverted exhaust valves. Primary and final drive by chain set the Indian apart from the multitude of belt-drive bikes. The countershaft-mounted gearbox started a trend away from gears in the rear hub. Indian/Finn

brisk for the era, and absolute reliability—all of which defined the product as excellent. A fourth key to success was the good management of the master organizer George Hendee and master designer Oscar Hedstrom.

A decade later, Hendee and Hedstrom knew there wasn't going to be a "motocycle" for every man after all. American automobile production had risen from the 1901 output of 4,192 to the 1910 totals of 181,000 cars plus 6,000 trucks and buses. George and Oscar cried all the way to the bank. Indian output had grown from three machines in 1901 to 6,137 in 1910. So although Indian had only a market niche instead of the whole motorized world, the niche was constantly growing and its end was nowhere in sight.

The Hendee Manufacturing Company enjoyed one of its greatest seasons in 1911. As well as record-breaking sales of 9,763, the iron redskins won the famous Isle of Man Tourist Trophy (TT) race, set a new transcontinental record, dominated American board-track racing, and held all 121 speed and endurance records. In 1913 Indian reached its all-time highest production and profits of 32,000 machines and $1.3 million. Sales were spurred by the new Cradle Spring frame, a swinging arm rear suspension 40 years ahead of the trend. By then, most Indians were V-twins, for the sporting side of motorcycling had overtaken the practical side. Production and profits leveled off the next two years, but technical excellence continued through the 1915 season with the last of the

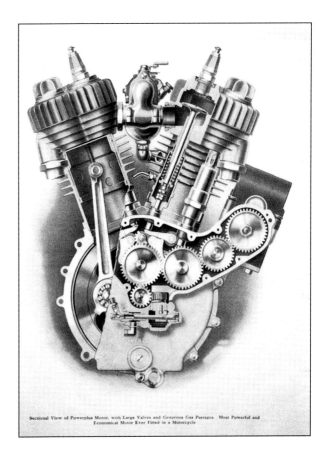

For 1916 Indian introduced Powerplus motors with all the valves on the side and total valve enclosure. The side-valve Powerplus motors were more powerful, quieter, and cleaner than the F-head motors they replaced. As in the F-heads, all valves are operated from a central two-lobe camshaft. A new feature is that cylinders and heads are one piece.

original engine concept, the so-called F-head (inlet-over-exhaust or IOE) machines with overhead inlet and side exhaust valves. These brought to the scene the first three-speed Indian transmission, generators for battery lighting, and other detail advances.

A new line of models debuted in 1916, the Powerplus line, featuring engines with all the valves on the side. The Powerplus models retained the styling of the preceding F-head range, but their side-valve engines were a radical departure from the industry norm. Initially, buyers greeted the Powerplus models with skepticism, but the engine lived up to its name by supplying more power, so the tide was turned.

Meanwhile, the American motorcycle industry and the American automobile industry were charting different courses. From 1913 through 1915, American car production grew 69 percent; Ford

The "cradle spring frame," shown here on a 1918 Powerplus, was used from 1913 through 1924 on some models. Although the design was about 40 years ahead of its time, competitors argued that the rear suspension was hard on chains. As with the earlier F-heads, the primary drive chain was covered by sheet metal. Jimmy Hill collection, via Earl Bentley (hereafter, "Hill/Bentley")

production tripled, rising to 450,000 cars. The American motorcycle industry stayed about the same over the three years, but Indian wasn't keeping pace. The production of industry leader Indian fell 35 percent, and Harley-Davidson production grew only 2 percent over the same interval.

The United States entered World War I in April 1917, and the motorcycle industry found it more difficult to sell to a shrinking crowd of available young men. Young men who stayed at home faced uncertainty in their civilian status, a prospect that demotivated them as buyers. Dealers also were not motivated because of the risky prospect of satisfactorily completing credit sales contracts. Dozens of motorcycle companies gave up the game. Indian made a lot of money on army motorcycles over the next three years, but its heavy commitment to government contracts resulted in inadequate civilian production and marked the turning point in the sales war between Indian and the rapidly rising Harley-Davidson Company of Milwaukee, Wisconsin.

With the war over in late 1918, prospects were bright for the handful of motorcycle manufacturers that had survived. Incidentally, the factory took on the nickname "Wigwam" around this time, when the final expansions gave the floor plan the look of a giant letter *A*, or wigwam. The public's uplifted mood followed the "war to end all wars," and American business was sure to boom in answer to the needs of war-torn Europe. Young men who had either gone "over there" or had put their stateside lives on hold would again be looking for the

Pound for pound, the 1920 Scout was among the most successful designs ever built. Most roads were unpaved, so the Scout's 50-mile-per-hour-plus top speed meant Scout riders of the era could usually ride as fast as safety would permit. The engine and transmission were bolted together as a single unit, and settled within a strong double-tube main frame. All of these features were retained in the later Chiefs. Hill/Bentley

Another Scout feature carried on with the Chiefs was the helical-gear primary drive, running in an oil bath and enclosed by a cast-aluminum housing.

adventure of motorcycling.

To gain a much-needed shot in the arm, Indian made a bold gamble. The company began engineering a radically different motorcycle, and it was ready for the 1920 season. The 37-cubic-inch (600-cc) middleweight V-twin was called the Scout. The Scout was a gamble because its many advanced features meant production cost was inevitably high, yet the model was to sell for a middle-range price in order to compete successfully.

The Indian gamble had an uncertain outcome. The immediate flood of Scout sales slowed after a few months, and total 1919 sales failed to reach 20,000. Still, Indian outproduced Harley-Davidson.

Unfortunately, the American economy suffered a severe downturn during the latter part of 1920, and Indian's sales fell below 14,000. By the time of the business slowdown, Indian was already committed to going double-or-nothing by following the Scout with a larger model along the same line.

Meanwhile, Harley-Davidson was overtaking

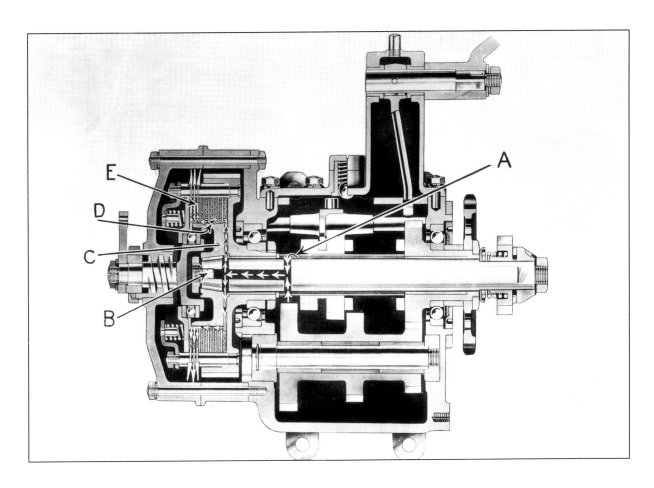

In the Indian transmission, shifting was accomplished by sliding the double-gear along the splined main shaft. In this picture, the transmission was in neutral. The left position was low; the middle position (slightly to the right) was second; the right position was high. In high, the power flow bypassed the triple gear. In low and second, the double-gear teeth meshed with the triple-gear teeth—not a good feature because of the wear and danger of breaking a tooth. Indian used the sliding-gear layout on all Chiefs. Indian/Finn

Indian on the race tracks, with back-to-back wins in the 1919 and 1920 Marion (Indiana) 200 road races (the only two years of this event) and a win in the 1920 Dodge City 300, the nation's premier motorcycle road race. These were the days when Harley-Davidson staffed a large team of top-notch salaried riders and backed this up with superlative team organization and continuous engineering studies. At stake were both racing and production preeminence.

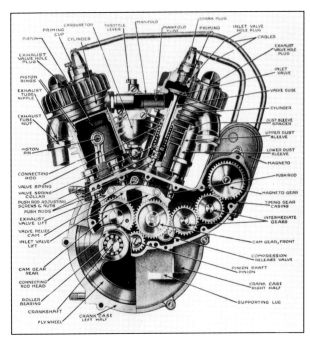

The next step in engine evolution was the 1920 37-cubic-inch (600-cc) Scout. The Scout motor featured two camshafts to operate the side valves, each camshaft working both valves of its dedicated cylinder. The webbed or open flywheel was typical of the era. The later Chief engine was basically an enlarged Scout unit.

Chapter 2

Chiefs of the Roaring Twenties
1921–1929

Following the economic downturn of late 1920, hope began to rise again. In late 1921, our Unknown Soldier of World War I was buried in Arlington National Cemetery, President Harding pleaded for a ban to war, and former President Wilson basked in public acclaim for his efforts that led to the ongoing international armaments-limitation conference. Americans fervently hoped and believed the sacrifices in Flanders' fields were not in vain and that the recent world war had proven the futility of armed conflict.

For 1922–1926 each cylinder head was built as a unit with its cylinder. The nickel-plated cylinders were standard for 1922–1931 and 1935–1942. The spark-plug base and the dome over the exhaust valve were removable, permitting valve removal and valve-seat grinding. The small starter-gear oiling hole in the chain guard was a 1926 feature.© Hans Halberstadt

The late-1924 Chief had a new pull-action front fork (that is, the springs pull upward on the rockers). The hand-shift lever had a round cross section. The handgrips shown were 1922–1926 issue. This "Princess" sidecar was used from 1922 through 1934.

Optimism went beyond the diplomatic sphere, infiltrating the thinking of families, breadwinners, small and large businesses, and, of course, the Hendee Manufacturing Company. There was only one way to go, and that was up.

1922: The First Chief

Against this backdrop, Indian's new heavyweight, the 1922 Chief, went on sale over the 1921 Labor Day weekend. This was a new kind of big motorcycle, big but not too big. The idea was to pit its 61-cubic-inch (1,000-cc) displacement and advanced specifications against larger twins from Harley-Davidson and Excelsior.

Basically, the Chief was an enlarged Scout. At the front was a trailing-link leaf-spring fork of the style used since 1910, but from there back, everything derived from the 1920 Scout.

The Chief engine was of side-valve layout, a type pioneered by Reading-Standard in late 1906 and used by Indian since the 1916 debut of the Powerplus. The Chief engine was similar to that of the Indian Powerplus still in production, but the Chief engine differed in valve-gear actuation. The Chief used two camshafts, one beneath each cylinder, and each camshaft operated both valves for the applicable cylinder. The older Powerplus design used a single centrally mounted camshaft that operated all four valves. A compression ratio of about 5:1 and mild valve timing restricted maximum engine speed to about 4,000 rpm and produced a maximum of

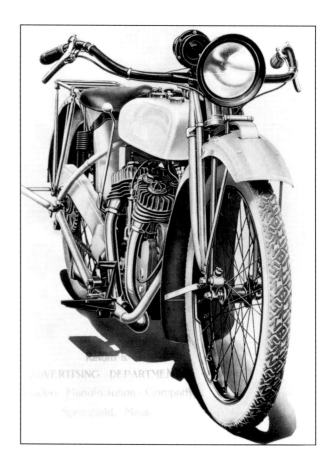

The 1922 Chief was the first of the tribe. The flat-sided gearshift lever was a 1922–1923 item. The compression release mechanism was operated by the hand lever on the left handlebar on the 1922 Chiefs only. Also unique to the 1922 domestic model were the standard equipment luggage rack and the auxiliary rear brake, operated by the right hand-lever. These items were used in later years on export models. Hill/Bentley

The early-1924 Chief still had a push-action fork. The enclosed saddle springs were used on 1924 and 1925 Chiefs. There was no auxiliary rear brake, so there was no hand lever on the right handlebar. Beginning in 1923, the compression release was mounted on the tank, so there was no hand lever on the left handlebar. Hill/Bentley

about 20 horsepower at the crankshaft. Top speed was about 65 miles per hour. Acceleration was helped by a total weight of 425 pounds, which was 150 pounds less than the 1953 Chiefs, the last to be produced. A standing-start quarter-mile run would probably have netted the rider about 55 miles per hour through the trap and an elapsed time of about 20 seconds. Though very mild by today's standards, Chief performance was typical of the era.

The Chief had an integrated powerplant that consisted of the engine and transmission bolted together. Power was transmitted from the engine to the transmission by helical gears running in a cast-aluminum oil-bath case. The arrangement was compact, robust, and clean running. In contrast, rival big twins had a separate engine and transmission connected by a sheet-metal-covered primary drive chain. On each rival, considerable

From the first, the Chief was billed as a sidecar hauler, while the smaller Scout was termed the ideal solo mount ("solo" meant two wheels instead of three). Early sidecar rigs were more sociable than today's three-wheelers because the passenger sat about as high as the rider.

twisting loads existed because the engine and transmission pulled each against the other, and the stamped-steel front chain cover was a guaranteed oil leaker.

To explain the good points of the Chief frame, let's first look at how Indian's main rival, Harley-Davidson, built its large motorcycles. On the big Harleys, the engine and transmission were separately attached to brackets that were fitted to a single lower tube beneath the motorcycle. This worked because chain primary drive compensated for the inevitable slight misalignment of the separate engine and transmission. Indian's other big rival, Excelsior, used a similar layout but fitted larger front and rear engine brackets in order to dispense with the frame tube beneath the engine. Because the layout of the big Harleys and Excelsiors produced a lot of twisting stress, riders had to keep a watchful eye on all the engine and transmission mounting bolts and nuts.

The Chief "cradle" frame was so named because two lower tubes, one on each side, cradled the powerplant between them. These two tubes started at the steering head and extended downward side by side for several inches before branching apart to form the left- and right-side lower tubes. The Chief powerplant sat in the double-tube frame almost as simply as a table sits on a floor, but instead of four "legs" the powerplant had three, like a camera tripod. The front of the powerplant was suspended from two mounting brackets, one on each side, and the rear was secured by a single through-bolt through the transmission case. Four-legged tables and chairs sometimes rock back and forth because they have a short leg, but a tripod never wavers on its perch, and the Chief mounting system was equally firm.

Over the telegraph lines came glowing endorsements of the new Chief by veteran Indian dealers. Here are a couple of them:
• "Chief arrived and has taken town by storm; riders of all makes like it; accept congratulations; rush September quota."
• "Indian chief announcement has spread like wildfire; riders and dealers all over the state are anxious for the arrival of stock for delivery."

Indian Dealers Favor the Scout Over the Chief

Indian published a series of weekly sales promotion pamphlets called *Contact Points* and distributed one copy to each Indian dealer.

From *Contact Points* No. 8, November 15, 1921: "The 1921 motorcycle and bicycle show is now history. As usual, the Indian exhibit was second to none on the floor. In fact, the center of attraction at the entire show was the beautiful Indian Chief and Princess side car finished in gold and white with red upholstering. But despite the approval of the new models, the fact remains that the Indian Scout held the center of the stage from the standpoint of Indian dealer interest."

To the Hendee outfit, the Scout and the Chief were the waves of the future that would render obsolete the old Indian Powerplus, as well as the Harley-Davidson and Excelsior big twins. The Scout and the Chief, after all, had side-valve engine design, a design that had proven superior to the F-head in British and European racing. Moreover, the new Indians also featured the markedly superior helical-gear primary drive and semi-unit construction. Yes, these were expensive motorcycles to build and that squeezed the profit margins, but could the motorcycling public resist such advanced models?

There was a fly in the ointment. Stunningly, Harley-Davidson won every national championship race of the 1921 season. Although Indian side-valvers had shown impressive speeds, and important race wins were just around the corner for Indian, Harley-Davidson had captured the speed image at a critical time in the industry.

Why Indian Liked Side-valve Motors and Why Its Rivals Would Follow Suit

As with the Scout, the Chief engine featured inverted side-by-side valves off to the right side of the cylinder bores, and thus the engine had a side-valve layout. Later the terms "L-head" and "flathead" were used to describe the type. Of the several desirable attributes of the Chief, the most important was this side-valve engine. On this score, Indian was looking more clearly into the future. In the United States, Indian was early on the side-valve scene, and would steer its rivals this way over the next several years.

The side-valve configuration was attractive because it avoided the mess that was common on F-head and overhead-valve engines resulting from their exposed overhead valves and rockers (the intakes only on F-head motors, but both intakes and exhausts on overhead-valve motors), as well as the reliability problems stemming from the open-air mixing of dust, oil, and moving parts, such that dust was ground into grinding compound and metal was ground into dust. Exhaust valves were high-failure items. For this reason overhead-valve and F-head engines of the era exposed their valves to the cooling air. With overhead-valve motors, you had twice as many messy and high-wearout parts as you had with F-head motors. On top of that (pun intended), an exhaust-valve failure could be catastrophic because the valve head was likely to drop into the combustion chamber and lock up the works. This wasn't a problem with the old F-head twins or the new side-valve twins because a broken exhaust valve would stay out of the way over in the so-called pocket at the side of the cylinder.

Although Indian chose the side-valve configuration for its new Chief and Scout engines primarily because of the side-valve's simpler more fully enclosed valvetrain and the resulting greater reliability, the side-valve proved to be a performer as well. The Indian side-valve motors soon stunned the motorcycling world by proving faster than the Indian and Harley eight-valve OHVs, as well as the Excelsior F-head racers. Indian won 14 of the 17 national championship races in 1920. Most notable was a race near Cleveland, Ohio, where Albert "Shrimp" Burns set a 10-mile record, averaging about 75 miles an hour while running against Harley-Davidson eight-valve overheads. These side-valve racing victories reinforced Indian's party line: Side-valve motors were the best combination of speed and proven reliability.

Side-valve racing success was also happening across the Atlantic, where Norton and Sunbeam racing motorcycles were the pacesetters. Of course, the Indian Chief wasn't designed to be a racer. Yet looking at the Chief design in 1922 with a perspective from that era, you couldn't say there was any hint of inferiority in the Chief engine design. The side-valve configuration was state-of-the-art stuff in the 1920s.

Hopping Up 1922 Motors

The factory offered special parts for extra speed in Scout, Chief, Standard (formerly Powerplus), and 72-cubic-inch (1,180-cc) models. The latter was a beefed-up Standard. For the Chief, the special parts consisted of aluminum pistons and associated cross-head pins for retaining the piston pin or little-end assembly. Also, the souped-up Chiefs got different inlet and exhaust valve hole plugs, which protruded into the combustion chamber and therefore raised the compression ratio. Another high-performance variant was the use of valve springs from the 72-cubic-inch motor. Ignition timing of the high-performance Chiefs was also ad-

Specifications

Models	1922–1925 Chief; 1923–1925 Big Chief
Engine	Side-valve 42-degree V-twin
Bore and stroke	
Chief	3 1/8 x 3 31/32 inches
Big Chief	3 1/4 x 4 7/16 inches
Displacement	
Chief	60.88 cubic inches (998 cc)
Big Chief	73.62 cubic inches (1,206.50 cc)
Horsepower (est.)	
Chief	25
Big Chief	30
Carburetor	Schebler, HX-180 (standard), DLX-4 (optional)
Lubrication	Total loss
Oil Pump	Separate body screwed to cam case cover*
Ignition	Magneto
Transmission	Three-speed, sliding-gear engagement
Clutch	Multiplate, wet
Primary drive	Helical gears in oil-bath case
Wheelbase	60 1/2 inches
Wheels and tires	27 inches (outside diameter) x 3.85 inches
Suspension	Front, leaf spring; rear, none
Weight	425 pounds
Saddle	Indian Special Suspension (apparently a Messinger Air Cushion)
Saddle height	30 inches
Miles per gallon	35–45
Top speed (est.)	
Chief	65 miles per hour
Big Chief	70 miles per hour

* *Note:* I use the term "cam case" for the valve instead of the Indian term "gear case" to avoid confusion with the traditional British term "gearbox," the latter being the set of gears Americans call the transmission. Beginning in 1936, Indian also used the term "cam case."

vanced. Ignition timing in those days was expressed in the amount of piston travel remaining before top-dead-center position. Both the fully advanced and fully retarded ignition timings were 3/16 inch earlier.

Cops Like the 1922 Chief

The Chief became the favored model of police departments using Indians. This testimonial from a motorcycle patrolman came from the March 31, 1922, *Contact Points:*

"Replying to your last letter to me asking me why I didn't tell you how I liked the Big Chief, will advise that I will have to expand my vocabulary as I do not possess the exact words. . . . I rode overtown Saturday afternoon and left the machine at the curb while I went after a smoke, but didn't have a chance to get it for a crowd soon gathered of about fifty or seventy-five persons, large and small, old and young, and you would naturally have thought I was a street faker [magician], but I was not. It certainly is the curiosity of the town and the best outfit yet."

In the first week of April, 29 of the 37 Indians sold to police were Chiefs.

1923: No Substitute for Cubic Inches

An important innovation for 1923 was Standard Oil's introduction of the fuel additive tetraethyl lead. Customers could buy the lead and add it

On top of the frame tube, the ammeter and light switch rode in their own box. From front to rear were the auxiliary oil hand pump, the fuel cap with integral removable primer syringe, the knurled fuel shutoff knob, and the compression release ("through the tank" 1927-1929). © Hans Halberstadt

to their tanks. The significance of leaded fuel was that overhead-valve engines could be operated with higher compression ratios, which in turn meant the overheads could produce significantly more power. This set the stage for the eventual dominance of overhead-valve engines, though overhead valves were still over a decade away in standard American motorcycles.

Despite some outstanding side-valve racing speeds, Indian found itself outpaced in the racing world of 1922 by the more consistent Harley-Davidson victories. As Indian entered the 1923 season, Harley-Davidson was the new number one in racing and the new number one in the showrooms. As good as the 61-cubic-inch Chief was, Indian needed something better.

A bigger Chief was the Wigwam's response. Harley-Davidson had taken the smarter road in 1921 with its first 74-cubic-inch big twin. So to hell with being smaller but better, we will just be better, the Wigwam reasoning went. For the 1923 season Indian brought out an enlarged Chief dubbed the

Big Chief, with the engine displacing 73.62 cubic inches, or 1,206.50 cc, and nominally billed as 74 cubic inches.

Indian introduced numerous updates and improvements to the Chief design for 1923. The Chief and Big Chief had a new pinion (timing gear side) shaft and pinion (timing) gear. A compression-release pull rod was mounted to the side of the right tank. The engine breathed through a different carburetor manifold that had new cones—the annular connectors between the manifold proper and the inlet nipples (ports) on the cylinders. The upper left and right rear fork tubes were joined by a tubular crossbrace, and the lower fork tubes were made of heavier stock. Detail changes were made to the automatic oiler, these being a different worm gear and a different plunger driver block. At the rear of the motorcycle, the single brake operated with an internal contracting band. The brake drum enclosed the works, lessening the entry of dust and moisture, elements that drastically reduced the effectiveness of the era's stoppers.

From the Indian sales and dealer promotional literature of the era you would think that most Indians were Scouts, but that was a reflection of Indian's sales philosophy rather than the relative strengths of the Scout and Chief models. The 74-cubic-inch Big Chief immediately took over as Indian's most popular model. The reason Indian stressed Scouts was the belief that the smaller V-twin did missionary work, bringing into the sport people who might otherwise pass it by. Management believed Scout owners could be sold Chiefs later.

Indian pitched the side-valve engine as the standard of the automotive industry. The company was telling the truth. Of 356 cars exhibited at the 1923 New York Automobile Show, 209 had side-valve engines. But although 58 percent of the show cars had side-valves, a more telling point was the Ford Model T. That universal car was spilling out into every corner of the nation, putting Americans on wheels, wheels turned by a side-valve motor.

Chiefs continued to be popular with police departments. During 1923 the Los Angeles Police Department bought 64 Chiefs and the Pennsylvania Highway Patrol bought 100 Big Chiefs. Of departments using Indians, the 74-cubic-inch Big Chief was by far the most popular model, and over three-fourths of factory police orders typically went to this type.

In November 1923 came the announcement that the company name had been changed from

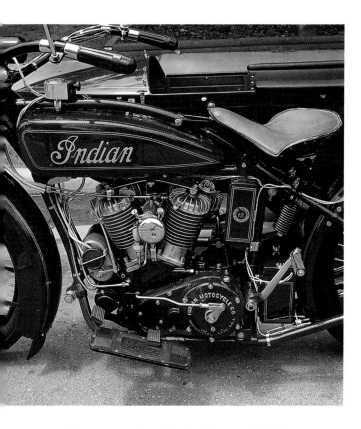

On late-1924 models, the clutch-housing label changed from "Hendee Manufacturing Co." to "Indian Motocycle Co." The left-side kickstarter was standard for 1922–1931 domestic models and fits in well with the Chief's primary use as a sidecar machine. All 1922–1931 Chief frames featured the front down tubes bending at the bottom to form integral horizontal and lower rear tubes. The "stretched leather bucket" Messinger saddle debuted in 1926, and starting that year, seat-post suspension was omitted.

Hendee Manufacturing Company to Indian Motocycle Company. The company would always continue to preach the facts and folklore of old George Hendee and fellow cofounder Oscar Hedstrom, but Hendee and Hedstrom had been gone since 1916, and it was time to move on.

1924: A Softer Chief Ride

Tetraethyl lead caught on rapidly as a fuel additive. In 1924, for the first time, a customer could buy leaded gasoline right from the pump instead of having to pour the additive into the tank. Henry Ford drove the stake deeper into the heart of motorcycling by selling the ten millionth Ford. The first Chryslers were put on the market.

For 1924, Indian concentrated on improving the Chief's ride. From the beginning of that season, the Chief was equipped with larger cross-section and lower-pressure tires, the so-called balloon

tires. In the middle of the 1924 season a "pull-action" front fork was put on the Chief and Big Chief (see illustrations). A shorter connecting link joined the rockers and the springs, which had the effect of angling the rockers more steeply upward. For a while, the new fork was offered at a special price for riders who wished to convert their earlier Chiefs. With the new fork came a new front fender.

The automatic oiler body was changed, but the complete oiler assembly continued with the same part number. The body featured an inlet boss that was horizontal instead of angled 45 degrees downward. The oiler also had a different worm gear, and Indian claimed the pump was enlarged, implying greater output.

The clutch release foot lever had a fold-up heel pad that prevented damage during a fall. A longer clutch actuating arm was fitted to achieve a more gradual engagement. A different worm release mechanism and thrust release ball bearing race also debuted. The clutch pedal mounting bracket was strengthened. Chiefs shipped after May 1 were fitted with a gasket between the primary drive case and the drive cover. The transmission case cover was new (details unknown), and there was no breather on top of the shifter tower.

The kickstarter was longer and worked with a 28-tooth starter pinion instead of a 24-tooth pinion. Both changes made the kicking chore easier. The luggage rack (accessory) had a different mounting style, being clipped to the rear fender proper instead of the rear fender braces. For 1924, the single rear brake (of domestic models) was fitted with two fabric facings in place of the former continuous single facing. This was claimed to reduce chatter and drag. The rear stand had an I-shaped cross section instead of a C-shaped cross section.

The First "B" Motors

Since 1922 (and possibly earlier) the Wigwam had advertised parts that dealers could install in order to make Chiefs, Scouts, and Standards run faster. Beginning in 1924 the factory did all the work by building to custom order extra-fast Big Chief and Scout motors. These "B" motors featured aluminum pistons (instead of iron). Other changes were made but weren't widely publicized. For example, one can confirm from the Indian service literature that later Scout "B" motors used the same larger carburetor as used on the Big Chief. All "B" motors were assembled off-line by designated technicians, and extra care was taken in the matter of clearances and tolerances. Clearances were looser throughout to reduce the likelihood of seizure un-

This 1926 Chief engine has the standard red-painted crankcase, transmission case, and primary-drive housing that were used on all 1922 through early-1926 Indians. The red paint was applied by dipping so the paint surface was uneven and the coarseness of the aluminum showed through. Beginning in February 1926, customers could opt for a powerplant without the red paint, in what Indian called a "brush" finish. Indian/Finn

der the expected high-speed running. Thus began a long tradition of factory hop-ups that eventually moved through the motor names of, Savannah, Daytona, and Bonneville.

1925: Another Tribal Rival

Elated by the continuing popularity of the Scout, Indian's management decided an even lighter and easier-handling model would further strengthen the line-up. The new entry was a 21.35-cubic-inch (350-cc) side-valve one-cylinder model called the Prince.

The Prince absorbed scarce engineering time and money that otherwise might have gone to the most popular model in the Indian line-up, the Big Chief 74. Pity the Big Chief. Although it was the biggest moneymaker from the Wigwam, it wasn't even second in the hearts of management. The unofficial but real pecking order was Scout, Prince, and Chief.

As ever, the nation's highway system continued to slowly evolve. During the year, the uniform federal highway numbering system was adopted. But it's one thing to have a numbering system and an-other thing to ensure adequate supplies of road signs are actually posted. Posting of highway signs didn't become universal for over a decade.

Chief Changes

On both the 61- and 74-cubic-inch versions, different inlet and exhaust pushrods were provided. A new combination of clutch plates was used, but the clutch and transmission assembly part number wasn't changed. This happened repeatedly during the 1920s. Also in the clutch, a Timken roller bearing replaced the earlier ball bearing. To improve brake operation, factory engineers came up with a different heat-treating procedure for brake linings. Chief brakes had previously suffered from an oily vapor emitted from the linings under severe braking conditions. To provide for cooler brakes, three 3 1/2-inch-diameter holes were drilled in the brake arm (backing) plate and in the brake drum.

1926: A Beefier Engine and External Changes

The 1926 Chiefs were the first in the series to include substantial internal changes. You can make a case either way as to what was the meaning of going through the first four years with so few technical changes. Surely this suggests that the original design was sound, but the lack of engineering updates also suggests that the Wigwam was resting on its laurels.

For 1926, Chief engines were fitted with revised drive-and-pinion shafts. As a result of the changes to the shafts, the Chief engine also sported new flywheels and bushings for the connecting-rod roller bearings. In addition, a "new" spring for both inlet and exhaust valves was fitted. This actually was a leftover Powerplus part. For dealers desiring faster Chiefs, special cams were offered.

Time for a definition. Indian often phased in changes during a model year. I call these "running changes" because the assembly line wasn't stopped and restarted as was the case with major cosmetic items. So, as a running change on the 74-cubic-inch Chief, new pistons were fitted. Each had a 3/4-inch wrist pin instead of a 5/8-inch wrist pin (these were called cross-head pins by Indian). Another running change saw "Drain Oil" rings and different oil control rings incorporated to improve oil circulation.

After this surge of Chief development, Indian engineering ignored the Chief for the next several years. Engineering resources instead were concentrated on the Scout and the upcoming four-cylinder models. By resting on its Chief laurels, Indian was making another of its long-term strategic mistakes.

On each cylinder head was a priming cup. These were to aid in starting the machine in cold weather. The rider unscrewed these about one-half turn, unseating the cup, then removed the priming pump from the tank filler cap and injected some fuel. The idea was not mainly to enrich the mixture (which does help). The main benefit was that the gasoline thins out the sticky oil on the piston and cylinder walls. Indian/Finn

Scout Love Affair Continues

While the 61- and 74-cubic-inch Chiefs soldiered along more or less as the profit-making equals of the Scout, Indian continued to emphasize the smaller V-twin as a better recruiter for new motorcyclists. By this time the Scout had taken on a somewhat cult status among dealers. These experienced motorcyclists appreciated the smaller model's subtle advantages of superior handling and versatility. Sincerity helped Scout sales, which lately were growing faster than Chief sales. The factory termed the Scout "the ideal and universal solo machine." ("Solo" meant no sidecar.)

Most police departments of the era were loyal to one of the three major brands, choosing either Indian or Harley-Davidson V-twins or the Henderson four-cylinder for use throughout the jurisdiction. An unusual development was the acceptance of the 37-cubic-inch (600-cc) Scout as a police motorcycle. With single-brand loyalty widespread among departments, Scout police sales in effect robbed sales from the Chief. In spring 1926, for example, the Pennsylvania Highway Patrol purchased 50 Scouts

and 26 Chiefs, a reversal of the usual Chief dominance.

In late 1926, the arrival of the 1927-model 45-cubic-inch (750-cc) Scout 1926 meant further reductions in sales of the Chief to police. The advertising department immediately made this police pitch: "Have you demonstrated the 45 to Police Departments? Do not overlook that the 45 will be announced and featured as the Police Special. . . . The Indian Scout 45 fits into police service like no other motorcycle ever has because it is designed particularly for what police departments at the present time require. . . . The average motor cop, if he speaks frankly, will tell you that it is a tiresome job to ride a big, heavy machine solo day in and day out. Therefore, he will positively welcome a machine which has all of the easy riding and easy handling qualifications of the Scout with the added pep and acceleration incorporated in the new 45. . . ."

In autumn 1926, the Chief finished its first five years on the market. The model started with a bang, then sales fell because of the general decline in the motorcycle industry and because the Chief had to compete with the very popular Scout. Internal rivalries were about to be intensified.

1927: A New Prima Donna and More Scout Competition

In January 1927 came a major development that would have far-reaching impact on the future of the Chief. Indian bought the manufacturing rights and tooling of the defunct Ace motorcycle company. The addition of the in-line four-cylinder Ace to the Indian line-up meant still more in-house

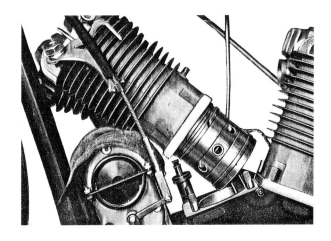

Shown in this service literature is a holed "hour glass" piston and thick piston rings that were typical of the era. Note that the cylinders and heads were cast as one piece for 1922–1926 Chiefs.

On this 1929 Chief, and all others for 1922 through 1931, the accessory speedometer was offset to the left. Beginning in 1927, the front fender had the spring connecting links outside the fender instead of running through it. The front brake debuted in mid-1928.

competition for the Chief, in the showrooms and in those police departments that already were Indian-exclusive. On the positive side, the Ace could also be expected to draw both regular and police sales away from the Henderson Four.

The factory made clear the Chief's falling status in Indian advertising with these words: "Very close to the Scout is the new Indian Scout 45, universally known as 'The Police Special.' This model has all the unique solo riding qualities of the Scout, plus the power, acceleration, and speed of the Indian Big Chief 74. . . . The Indian Scout 45 has all the bearcat getaway of the Indian Big Chief—PLUS—all the economy, smoothness, and ease of handling of the Indian Scout."

So just what was the Chief supposed to offer if, one, it wasn't the top-of-the-line glamour wagon, and two, it wasn't any faster or quicker off the line than the Scout 45? The Chief and Big Chief had only one trick left; they were the best of the tribe for pulling a sidecar. Yawn.

Chief Developments

The valve lifter (compression release) was relocated inboard from the side of the tank so that the lifter rod passed through a cylindrical channel or "dummy hole" in the tank and the lifting knob was protruding from the top of the tank. Each tank-side decal bore the added legend "Chief" in small block letters below the Indian script. The Splitdorf NS-2 magneto designation had a distinctive cross pattern on the end cap.

"New" front and rear connecting rods for the 61-cubic-inch and 74-cubic-inch Chiefs were actually a running change made on late-1926 Chiefs. The right and left crankcases provided increased oil-sump capacity to reduce power-robbing crankcase compression.

In the clutch, a combination of six plain and three grooved raybestos driver plates replaced the previous eight plain raybestos driver plates. The transmission main shaft was changed. This was the same change applied to Scouts and consisted of a main-shaft end plug that diverted oil circulation to the clutch plates. Dealers were provided modification instructions to convert earlier Chiefs.

Remember the Pennsylvania Highway Patrol's order for 50 Scouts in 1926? These 37-cubic-inch Scouts were used throughout the winter of 1926–1927 attached to sidecars, the use that was the supposed specialty of the Chiefs. The 1926 37-cubic-inch Scouts proved so good that, late in 1927, the highway patrol ordered 50 more Scouts; these were probably 45-cubic-inch models. To yet another degree, the Chief was marginalized.

1928: The Full Line

Indian proudly claimed "the full line" for 1928, with offerings of a single, small and large twins, and a four. This was their first full-line literature because the four came on the scene during the 1927 season and as, originally, the Ace. It was also the only year that it could advertise such a range of models because 1928 was the last year of the Prince single.

The Chief headlight was larger and the rim was nickel-plated instead of black. The semi-sport handlebars had different handlegrips. A new horn button had the base plate screwed into the handlebars. This replaced the clamped-on 1927-only toggle switch with internal contacts. Mounted to the front fork and just behind the handlebars was the new instrument panel that was used on all models. The Westinghouse induction ammeter bore the face legend "Westinghouse Use 2 Turns." As indicated, behind the face two wire loops were formed in lieu of traditional wire connections. The Westinghouse ammeter was used through 1934. The Splitdorf DU-7 generator was introduced on all models. The electric-motor-driven (ooga) horn became a standard feature. The horn was moved to the left side beneath the tank.

New cylinder heads had higher compression and yielded higher top speed, although the exteriors were unchanged. The crankcase breather was relocated to the left forward edge of the crankcase, near the clutch pedal. This may have been a running change on late-1927 models. The timing case cover was changed to accommodate the new oil pump that was fitted to the twins. The oil pump had a horizontal plunger. An oil shut-off line was added. The taillight featured a "solid" (not braided, not helical) cable casing.

Prior to 1928, Chief left and right flywheels were identical. On the 1928 74-cubic-inch model only, the right flywheel was new, and the reason for the change remains unknown. The remaining functional changes applied to both 61-cubic-inch and 74-cubic-inch models. A different right crankcase was required to accommodate a different pinion shaft; details are unknown. The left crankcase part number was changed because of the relocated crankcase breather. The rear cylinder was the same, but the front cylinder was changed to provide clearance for the new Splitdorf DU-7 generator.

The Chief clutch and transmission were made of improved alloys. Sixteen clutch spring studs were used instead of 12 studs. For the transmission drive gear, a ball bearing replaced the previous roller bearing that was used from 1925 through 1927 (1922 through 1924 Chiefs used a different ball bearing). A new rear brake featured an adjustable lower band.

From mid-1928, the Chief was redesignated the Series 301, in line with Indian's new policy of no annual models. The Series 301 Chiefs, like the Series 101 Scouts, Series 201 Prince single-cylinder, and Series 401 Four, were to be changed as im-

The unpainted "brush" finish of this 1929 motor, transmission, and primary-drive case began as a mid-1926 option. In 1927, removable cylinder heads debuted on the Chiefs, two years after their first use on the Scout and Prince models.

provements became available rather than waiting for the next year. At least that was the theory. In practice, the changes still tended to come annually, and today's collectors still refer to 1928, 1929, 1930, and 1931 models, the years in which theoretically there were no new annual models.

Midseason 1928 Chiefs, in common with the rest of the range, were outfitted with a front brake. The strengthened Chief fork main frame included a fixture for the telescoping brake anchor. The front fender was mounted to an inverted Y-shaped bracket, which in turn was suspended from the middle of the fork. The shape of the lower fender braces was changed. Shown in the June literature was a different muffler without a cutout.

1929: A Year of Few Changes

Drop-center rims replaced clincher rims. From June 1929, all carburetor bodies were die (pot or scrap) metal instead of cast. The regular handlebars had a different bend. All Chiefs shipped after April 12 were fitted with a clevis on the front end

Progress in Highways

Progress in the nation's highways had been steady but slow since the turn of the century. John L. Butler's book *First Highways of America* reports that the first concrete streets in the nation were installed back in 1891 in Bellefountaine, Ohio. But the expense of concrete kept it from being used for highways. In the early 1920s, only a tiny fraction of America's highway miles were paved. Almost all major highways were surfaced with gravel (smooth stones) or crushed rock (rough stones), and either way they all looked like gravel to motorists. But these "gravel" roads were of considerably varying quality. Good ones started with a deep trench into which stones of 2 or 3 inches in diameter were poured and then rolled. Above the base stones, middle-sized stones about 3/4 inch in diameter were laid and rolled. On top, the smallest stones were laid and rolled. Good "gravel" roads and bad "gravel" roads looked the same when they were both freshly laid. The difference was in the staying power of the surface. Some cheaply made gravel roads were little more than a sprinkling of gravel over unprepared dirt; consequently, rains and vehicles turned these so-called gravel roads into deeply rutted affairs.

Then, of course, there were the lesser roads. These were simply dirt trails, which after normal rains became impassible to wheeled-vehicle travel. In the early 1920s, there were a lot more miles of dirt roads than of gravel highways.

The progress of America's highways had a lot to do with the evolution of America's motorcycles. As highways improved, riders were able to ride faster and to ride fast longer. This hadn't happened yet in the early 1920s, but the future could be seen. A glimpse into the future was offered in 1922 when T. Coleman du Pont personally paid for the concrete pavement of du Pont Boulevard from Wilmington, Delaware, to the Maryland border, a distance of almost 100 miles.

The transportation revolution started by Henry Ford and his Model T worked its way from the cities into ever-more-remote rural areas. At about this time my father, Charles Hatfield, was six years old and living on a farm in Oklahoma. One day his mother called excitedly, "Come see this! You won't believe it!" The cause of the excitement? There were three Model T Fords in a row chugging down the dirt road. They had never seen three cars at the same time.

Although the Model T Ford was rapidly making motorists out of Americans, early-1920s road construction hadn't yet taken full advantage of motorized equipment. Motorcycles and cars were improving faster than roads, so engineering staffs weren't yet vitally concerned with reliability problems. Michael Karl Witzel

of the rear brake rod (which connected the brake to the cross shaft). All Chiefs shipped after July 15 (and some shipped before) were fitted with reshaped wheel hubs that spin on Timken roller bearings. The crankcase breather was moved to the cam case cover.

The Chief Becomes Obscure

The 1929 business year saw passenger car production reach the record level of 4.6 million. Just five years earlier, production had been 3.7 million, so the automobile industry five-year growth rate was 25 percent. Although the nation in general and the car builders in particular were enjoying boom times, the motorcycle industry had experienced no growth in the past five years. Production at Indian and Harley-Davidson remained fairly constant at about 50 percent of plant capacities. The loss of military sales after World War I coincided with the public's declining interest in motorcycles, that decline being mainly because of the newly affordable Ford Model T.

The Prince single wasn't in the 1929 line-up. Partly, the failure of the Prince was due to Harley-Davidson's simultaneous debut of their own 21-cubic-inch side-valve single. There just wasn't a big enough market for both companies to share this field. For the most part, the Prince had a negative

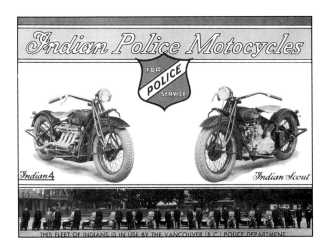

By the late 1920s, the Chief had become a low-priority model emphasized only for sidecar use. This centerfold from the October 1929 Indian News "Special Police Issue" shows that Indian was no longer billing the Chief as the ideal police mount.

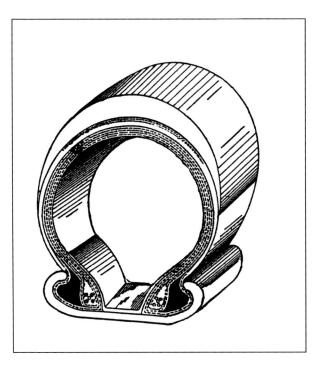

The worst of both worlds: Clincher tires, used until 1929, were very difficult to remove and replace. Conversely, if they were ridden underinflated or if a puncture or blowout happened, clincher tires usually left the rim, causing many a bad accident.

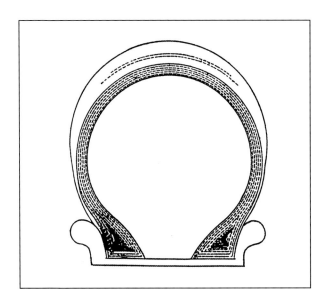

Modern "wired-on" tires came to motorcycling in 1929. The name was derived from the embedded reinforcing wire within the inner circumference. Working with the new tires were so-called drop-center rims, the same concept as used today. Air pressure tightly wedges the tire against the rim. These tires were more easily removed and replaced, yet almost never leave the rim when underinflated or when a blowout or puncture occurs.

impact because the lightweight absorbed scarce engineering time that, in retrospect, would've been put to better use on the Scout and Chief. The Four hadn't been so shortchanged because it was engineering's new baby, and in fact, a great deal of engineering effort had recently been given the Four.

By now, Indian's four-cylinder offering had completed its three-stage metamorphosis, as the 1927 Ace, the 1928 Indian Ace, and the 1929 Indian Four. With the Four billed as the last word in luxury and the 45-cubic-inch (750-cc) Scout as the ideal single-track all-arounder, the Chief soldiered on with the unglamorous mission of sidecar hauler.

What about police business, you ask? *Indian News* for October 1929 was dubbed the "Special Police Issue." There was a two-page centerfold. Large three-quarter profiles of the Indian Four and Scout appeared under the banner of "Indian Police Motorcycles."

So, the Chief was no longer the obvious choice for police sales. But as I've already said, there were other troubles for the big twin. It wasn't the top-of-the-line heavyweight; that role belonged to the four-cylinder Ace. The Chief wasn't the ideal fast road-burner; that job belonged to the Series 101 Scout. Like a man without a country, the Chief had become a motorcycle without a mission.

Chapter 3

Bottoming Out and Climbing Back *1930–1934*

In March 1930 E. Paul du Pont took over as Indian president. He inherited a mess, caused largely by an inner circle of managers who had been passing company money under the table to each other. Con artists, in other words. Mr. du Pont also inherited an engineering department that had spent the bulk of its time for the past three years trying to improve the reliability of the Four. The highly successful Series 101 Scout had required only scant attention, as the model was just a happy combination of specifications that spelled good reliability and performance. Engi-

neering updates to the Chief consisted mainly of oil pump updates in common with the 101 Scout. The combination of engineering scarcity and the

This handlebar-mounted instrument panel debuted on the 1928 Indians. The only full year of these cast-aluminum tanks was 1930, but some 1931 Chiefs have cast tanks. The external ammeter light was operated by pressing and turning. A simple twist switch operated the external light for the accessory speedometer.

The removable fuel injector pump was moved from the right fuel cap to the left fuel cap in 1932. The foot pedals were longer and wider, while the footboards were moved forward and were less steeply inclined. The separate front down tubes and main horizontal tubes were joined by malleable iron castings forward of the crankcase. The 4.00x18-inch tires on this 1932 Chief were standard for 1931–1939.

This 1930 Chief wears the correct 1927–1934 handgrips. The crankcase breather was on the left crankcase. The headlight rim and other small parts were chrome-plated, a midyear or "running" change. The 1931 models have the same profile, whether early units with cast-aluminum tanks or later units with sheet-metal tanks. Since this bike is ridden regularly, it's fitted with a 1940s-era air cleaner; stockers didn't have an air cleaner

sales department's pro-Four and pro-Scout advertising had allowed the Chief to fall ever further behind in the popularity contest with Harley-Davidson's big twins. The Chief, in short, had become a dog.

The Chief's problems could hardly have come at a worse time. The 4.6 million automobiles produced for the 1929 business year were a testimony to the general strength of the economy just prior to the stock market crash in October. But then car sales for business year 1930 fell to 2.8 million, a one-year drop of 39 percent! The Great Depression wasn't fully understood yet, but a major economic decline was obvious. The worst economic news was yet to come. So Chief neglect and bad times coincided.

1930: New Features and Problems

The 1930 Chiefs got cast-aluminum tanks. The crankcase breather was moved to the left crankcase, near the forward edge, and above the clutch pedal. Indian's first use of chrome trim occurred as a running change in early 1930. These were the bits and pieces formerly nickel-plated. Other running changes included heavy spokes for the front wheel, a larger headlight with different side brackets, and a new embossed headlight rim (also new in that it was chrome-plated). A flexible (helical wound) "armored" taillight cable was fitted. On November 25, the company announced that frame numbers had been initiated—earlier Indians had a motor number

only. (Note: the 1930 models were produced throughout 1930; the 1931 models were announced in March 1931.)

Chief Problems

Prior to du Pont's arrival, Indian took a misguided approach to closing the performance gap of the 1930 Chief compared to the Harley-Davidson big twins. Here's the story from Fresno, California, dealer Harold Mathewson:

"In 1930 they put out a high-compression 74 motor, but they didn't change the cylinders. All they did was put alloy pistons in with a spoked wheel [flywheel], cast-iron wheel. And after we had our dealers' meeting, boy, everybody boosted these new motors up, so that I ordered seven of them for March 1930. And I sold them real rapidly. I'd rolled out six of them, and I had one left. A customer came in the store, and I was selling him the last one that I had.

"So one of my customers that bought the one before, he'd just gone out [into] the alley, and he'd barreled it out fast. And I never thought anymore about it. Why, he came back to the store, walking, and he didn't say nothing. He walked in while I sold the last motorcycle, and the last buyer went out the front way and was gone. And then the next-to-the-last buyer says, 'Come on down in the alley. I want to show you something.' So I walked down the alley. Those flywheels had fallen apart with that high-compression alloy piston in there. It broke the crankcase and the transmission. And the flywheels fell out. Both cylinders [were] raised off it, and it was a mess. So we took a box down and picked up everything.

"We took it back, and we took it out of the frame. I had it there in a box. And it just happened that [Hap] Alzina [Indian's West Coast distributor] walked in the front door. I said, 'Hap, I have something that I want to show you.'

And he walked back there and he says, 'Oh! Put that under the bench! Put that under the bench!'. . . He did replace the motor, but several of those motors blew, one right after the other. I had to take every one, even those that didn't blow, and I took them down and put in a lower-compression piston. It cost me a thousand bucks besides all my labor."

By the way, a thousand bucks in 1930 would buy three new Indian twins. That was quite a bill for a young dealer to absorb.

Meanwhile, the company president, E. Paul du Pont, was checking out his wares. Here's a sample of what du Pont didn't like about the 1930 Chief, extracted from a July letter to his plant manager, Loren "Joe" Hosley.

"The vibration [of a Harley] is very much less, so much less, in fact that the Harley is quite us-

Beginning in 1929, there were standard colors other than red. Although this example is correct in its single-color finish, the 1930 standard color choices included colored tank panels, typically either cream or red. This was the last year for the style of oil pump used since the first 1922 Chiefs.

able, whereas the Indian Chief is not. To convince yourself of this, put the two machines side by side on a stand and start the motors. As they speed up, the Indian will be observed to vibrate so badly that it slides backward on the floor, and any attempt to hold it is painful to the hand; whereas the Harley stays more or less where it is placed at any engine speed. . . . The sitting position on the Harley is much more comfortable. . . . In general, I do not think our engineering is up to date in the matter of allowing our motors to churn up at maximum speed, and as high speed seems to be what is wanted, I think something might be done about this. . . ."

The Tampa, Florida, Indian dealer had even more harsh words for the Chief in a November letter to President du Pont: "If there is any possible chance, please give us a good 74 motor, and change the Chief to give it more speed, make the bottom of these motors so they will hold up. The crank pins, roller bearings, lower connecting rod bushings—it is fierce the way they go to pieces in no time. . . . I

found with our Indians, motors get too hot and too much vibration; front and rear brakes, no good; forks, too rough riding.

"Mr. du Pont, I have been selling motorcycles for 19 years and I know what I am talking about; I sold the Harley-Davidson fourteen years in this territory, and I know what they are made of and how they stand up. . . . If the Indian factory made a good 74 motor I could put them in the City and also in the County, but I cannot put the Chiefs in; the County men rawhide their motors, and I know the Chiefs will not stand up; I would just lose my reputation if I sold them, so I don't on that account. . . .

"Now what the Indian factory should do, is to make a 74 motor that will stand up, something to compete with the Harley-Davidsons. I am fighting a battle here, and have got to have more weapons to fight or give up, and I am one of the fellows that wants to die with his boots on.

"So please do all in your power to give us better production and especially on the Chief."

The dealer's letter only confirmed what du Pont already knew, for du Pont was a motorcyclist, a real one, not a public-relations dude. As a motorcyclist, he knew a dog when he rode one. E. Paul du Pont knew the Chief too well.

1931: Chiefs Redesigned

American rural roads continued to be improved, so that more and more stretches of straight going were found, along with more and more miles of well-graded gravel. This meant that the level of Chief performance that had been adequate in the old days had gradually become inadequate because of more and more high-speed running. In turn, this meant Chief deficiencies became more obvious and customer complaints more frequent.

New Chief internals were insisted on by du Pont, the new Indian president who agreed with complaining dealers and riders about the inadequate Chief performance, particularly rough running. To a large extent, the Chiefs needed substantial improvements because they had been neglected in favor of re-engineering the Four and the Scout.

The numerous internal changes on the 1931 Chiefs defined the most significant makeover of this model to date. The flywheels were "solid"; that is, they weren't webbed or spoked like all previous flywheels. The stronger flywheels, in combination with either light "special alloy" pistons or (new and lighter) cast-iron pistons, had a different balance factor, so the new configuration spelled smoother running. The optional alloy pistons ran with less clearance, which reduced running noise. Cast-iron pistons had a changed cross-head (wrist or gudgeon) pin that was retained by a lock ring instead of a dowel pin. Oil-control rings featuring two slots were announced January 1931 and were claimed to reduce oil consumption.

Early 1931 Chiefs continued with the cast-aluminum tanks that had debuted in 1930, but after stocks were used up, the tank construction reverted to sheet metal. In common with the rest of the line-up, the 1931 Chiefs got a lot of external changes. The most significant of these were Duco lacquer finish, cadmium-plated spokes, cadmium-plated fork top plate (which replaced the earlier left and right side "buttons" on the fork top), Indian-face horn, center-mounted headlight, handlebar crossbar, tank transfers with "74" in block style, throttle-controlled oil pump, muffler with cutout reinstated, serial number on frame (may have been 1930 running change), armored taillight wire (flexible instead of solid), heavy spokes on rear wheel, quickly detachable rear wheel, and internal rear brake.

The new rear brake forced the adoption of a 42-tooth rear sprocket as a replacement for the 36-tooth sprocket. To keep overall gear ratios proper, the primary drive had to spin the transmission faster without spinning the engine faster. The answer was a larger driver gear (39 teeth instead of 33) and smaller idler gear (36 teeth instead of 40) to work with the same clutch gear (84 teeth). The primary drive housing and cover appeared different because of the substantially larger front area around the larger drive gear.

1932: The New-Look Chief

In 1932, the Chief, Scout, and Four were drastically changed. The most visible change was a new look distinguished by frames with a taller front end, a longer fork, and "saddle" fuel tanks that draped over the top frame tube. Previously, only the Chief used tanks that shrouded the top frame tube. Although the Four frame was different to accommodate the differently shaped powerplant, the Four frame had the same relationship of steering head, tanks, saddle mounting, and footboards as did the Chief and Scout frames. This was a new deal, as previously the Chief frame was uniquely shaped within the line-up, while the earlier Scout and Four shared frame geometries. The Chief solo saddle height was lowered from 30 inches to 29 inches; buddy seat height was 31 1/2 inches. The wheelbase was extended from 60 1/2 to 61 1/2 inches. Weight (dry) climbed from 425 to 445 pounds. Also new was Dulux enamel, which replaced the 1931-only Duco lac-

On the 1931 Chief, the headlight was center-mounted directly to the handlebars. This was the first year for the Indian-face horn and the last year for the telescoping brake anchor and handlebar-mounted instrument panel. The muffler was a one-year-only design. The new total-loss oil pump, which varied output with throttle opening as well as engine speed, was used on 1931 and 1932 models only. This example has the cast-aluminum tanks, but later 1931 Chiefs had sheet-metal tanks. Hill/Bentley

quer that had proven fragile.

The new Chief frame had the two front downtubes widely splayed from the steering head instead of running parallel for much of the distance downward. The widely splayed downtubes were suggested by du Pont after observing that Four frames seldom went out of alignment after a crash, but earlier Chief and Scout frames often did. The stronger frame transferred the stress of accidents to the front fork, but it was easier to repair or replace a bent front fork than a bent frame.

Indian's basic sales pitch for the new-look Chief was brilliant, not to mention something of a turnabout on previous advertising that touted Scouts with the performance of Chiefs: the handling of the Scout coupled with the power of the Chief.

Said *Indian News* road tester Erle "Red" Armstrong: "It was an Indian 74 and yet it looked like an Indian Scout!. . . The new fork with its easier spring action and the new saddle and footboard position, all helped me realize right off the bat, that I was riding the most comfortable Indian I had ever been astride. . . . The more I rode this new model the more I was impressed with the fact that it has Indian 74 punch and getaway, with Indian Scout easy handling."

Along with the new Chief came two new models. A low-cost twin called the Scout Pony combined a 30.50-cubic-inch (500-cc) engine with the transmission, clutch, and running gear

A taller front end and new tanks give the 1932 Chief an entirely new look—"Scout looks and handling coupled with Chief power," proclaimed the Wigwam. The front spring leaves, connector link, and hub were wider than in previous years. The crankcase breather was newly situated on the forward part of the cam case cover. The three-piece exhaust system shown has two 1932-only features: a cast-iron connector between the front- and rear-cylinder exhaust-pipe sections and the muffler design. This was the first year the right gas tank had an independent reserve shutoff. The bent shift lever enabled gear shifting when carrying double. The shift knob was a period accessory.

of the defunct Prince single. This model stayed in production until World War II with two subsequent names, Junior Scout and Thirty-fifty. There was also a new Scout. But to the dismay of many Indian enthusiasts, the smaller motor was the only difference between the Chief and the new Scout. The identical frames of the Chief and the Scout were built in two variants, one for extension saddle suspension and the other for seat-post saddle suspension, the latter a first-time offering. The Scout/Chief frame was equipped with a Timken roller bearing for the lower steering-head section.

To cut costs, many Chief and Scout features were also used on the Four. Henceforth, Indian built these three models with as much commonality as possible. The following features applied to

For 1932 only, the standard ignition system circuit breaker was in front of the engine. The claw-shaped bracket supporting the hand-pump oil line and the ignition wiring was also unique to the 1932 models. Starting in 1932, the clutch pedal was mounted to the frame instead of to the primary-drive case.

The 1932 Chiefs were the last year with the flat headlight lens, and the first with the instrument panel clamped to the frame. In advertising photos like this, the front fender had incorrect lines in the lower area. Refer to the top photo on page 33 to see the correct fender. The primary-drive cover was larger on the front in order to house a larger drive gear, a change that took effect on the 1931 Chiefs. Hill/Bentley

each. The wheel hub, front fork, and leaf spring were each wider. The brake lever was moved closer to the right grip. The instrument panel was mounted to the frame, instead of the handlebars, via an integral clamp. The ammeter featured a 10-amp maximum indication and the legend "Westinghouse Use Two Turns," "TYPE BT," "AMPERES." The ignition switch incorporated a removable key. Previously only a simple rotary switch was provided.

On the Chief and the Scout, saddle suspension was either by the traditional external extension springs or by the new option of a seat post with internal telescoping springs; seat-post suspension wasn't offered on the Four. Optional saddle springs with lighter compression or with tension were offered. Also, the rear saddle support bracket had four adjustments for different ride qualities.

The tank filler caps were stainless steel instead of nickel-plated. Some tanks were decorated with a single narrow stripe about 3/64 inch wide, which outlined the tank in profile; other tanks had twin profile stripes of the same narrow width. On the Chief and Scout only, the oil compartment was moved to the front of the right tank along with the auxiliary hand pump. Previously, the oil compartment (in the right tank) had been behind the fuel compartment. With the relocated oil compartment came a different location for the auxiliary oil hand pump. The hand pump was just to the right of the oil-tank cap instead of in line with and between the fuel and oil caps. In the right tank, a "cofferdam" (space) was placed between the fuel and oil compartments that prevented a simple leak in the solder seal from allowing fuel and oil to mix.

"Half Roads and Motorized Road Construction"

Achieving a national paved highway system was a long struggle. *First Highways of America* by John Butler (Krause Publications, 1994) is a history of the nation's highway development. The book contains the following excerpt from a 1931 issue of the magazine Literary Digest:

"It is as foolish to build a twenty-foot road where a ten-foot one would do, as it would be to try to get along with the narrower one in heavy traffic. Best of all, halving the width doubles the length without extra cost; and in many rural regions, length, rather than width, is what is needed."

The advocated half-roads had one paved lane and one dirt lane and had been around since 1910 or so. The half-roads were an unusual way of compromising in the continuing struggle between advocates of improved roads and advocates of fiscal frugality.

Motorized road-construction equipment escalated the pace of highway construction during the 1930s. Roads were being improved faster than motorcycles. Faster riding for longer periods increased the engineering challenge to produce more reliable motorcycles. Michael Karl Witzel

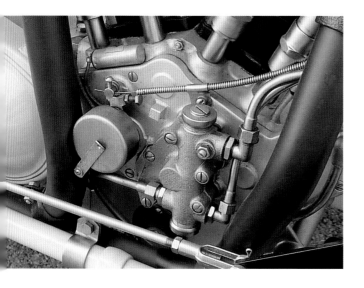

The 1933 Indian twins received the major improvement of dry-sump (circulating) lubrication. The dry-sump oil pump had a supply line (top front), a return line (bottom front), and a sump suction line (bottom rear). The dark circular cover behind the pump encloses the crankcase sump valve, where excess oil was sucked from the motor base. Just ahead of the rear exhaust pipe was the circular cover for the relocated standard battery-ignition circuit-breaker unit.

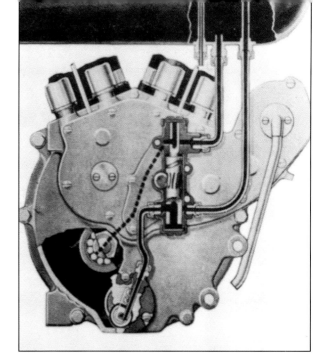

The major parts of the new 1933 dry-sump pump were the double-ended plunger for both feed and return pumping, and the sump valve in the bottom of the crankcase for scooping up excess oil. The double plunger was used on 1933–1937 Indian twins. Harley-Davidson waited until 1937 to incorporate dry-sump lubrication on all its models.

On the right side of the tanks a longer and differently shaped shift lever was fitted to the Chief and Scout. On the end of the lever was a removable hardrubber ball instead of the earlier integral metal ball. The factory first offered an optional left-side shift lever to be used with an optional right-hand throttle. This change was made to facilitate converting Harley riders into Indian riders (Harley-Davidson twins came standard with left-hand shift and right-hand throttle). Action of the Chief and Scout clutch foot pedal could also be reversed to achieve heel-down disengagement and "toe-to-go" action so beloved by Harley riders, despite its being the opposite of all automotive practice.

The Chief engine was changed in a number of ways. Early cylinder heads and cylinders were nickel-plated; later in the year, these were painted black. New cylinder heads had fore-and-aft cooling fins instead of radially disposed fins. Apart from the black finish, the Chief cylinders were unchanged from those of 1931. The three-piece exhaust system featured a cast-iron connector between the front- and rear-cylinder exhaust-pipe sections, in lieu of the previous two-piece system without a connector. A short fishtail-section tailpipe was attached directly to the upper rear of the muffler instead of to a long tailpipe attached to the center rear of the muffler.

For the first time since the diamond-frame era, magneto ignition was optional instead of standard. For the Chief and the Scout the new standard ignition system featured battery-powered sparks timed by a circuit-breaker device. In this case, Indian borrowed a leaf from the Harley-Davidson book because the optional battery ignition used the double-spark or wasted-spark system in which both spark plugs fire on each engine revolution. Harley-Davidson had long bragged about this layout because it avoided the use of a distributor, which Harley claimed was troublesome. The circuit breaker was mounted in the same place otherwise occupied by a magneto, and the breaker unit was driven by the same train of gears used for the magneto drive. The whole layout appeared to be the result of a hurry-up decision, as the opportunity hadn't been taken to eliminate the expensive gear train.

The other major item of the electrical system, the generator, was no longer out in front of the motor, gear-driven, and beneath the magneto. Instead, the generator was located beneath the saddle and was belt-driven from the rear of the primary drive case. The generator was an Auto-Lite unit instead of a Splitdorf. The generator belt guard was a one-year-only item because it mated with the one-

This 1933 Chief shows the correct headlight with a convex lens. Starting in 1933 the front-brake anchor was formed by a lever, and the muffler had a short fishtail section exiting the center instead of the upper rear. Black-painted cylinders were used on some 1932 and all 1933 and 1934 Chiefs. Black cylinder heads were also standard in the era. © Hans Halberstadt

year-only removable generator take-off drive at the rear of the primary drive case.

The footboards were moved forward and were inclined more steeply, and the foot pedals were longer. A long return spring was added to the brake pedal. A single rod joined the pedal to the operating lever on the brake drum, thus eliminating the previously required small bell crank between the front and rear rods.

A first-time feature was the standard right-side kickstarter, but riders still had the option of changing the starter to the opposite side. Since the right-side starter was standard, a revised standard chain guard was fitted; the revised guard had a cut-out area to accommodate the starter and was trimmed down over its whole length. Behind the kickstarter was the battery, as before, but the battery was out in the open instead of enclosed in a box. Securing the battery was a one-year-only inverted-U anchor strap. A new toolbox and toolbox location were featured. The Chief was now fitted with the same toolbox as the Scout (instead of boxes unique to each model). The toolbox was moved from beneath the saddle on the seat mast to a location behind the battery and on the left side of the rear tire.

The front part of the rear fender was secured to the upper rear fork crossbrace of the frame by a single, center-mounted, hat-shaped clamp; previously, this part of the rear fender was secured to the upper rear fork by a hat-shaped clamp on each side—at the two o'clock position on the right side and at the ten o'clock position on the left side.

More than 1,400 banks failed in 1932. The gross national product, the sum of all goods and services provided during the year, fell to $58 billion, less than half of the 1929 output. Automobile production totaled 1.1 million, less than one-fourth of the 1929 peak.

1933: Good Engineering but Empty Buildings

In early 1933, the Depression bottomed out when one of every four workers was unemployed. Then a modest upturn began. By year end, automobile production had risen to 1.6 million. While this was a 45 percent increase over 1932, the total was still only about one-third of the 1929 peak.

The giant Wigwam had once built 35,000 redskins in a single year. In 1933, Indian built only 1,667 motorcycles, less than 5 percent of production capacity! This was a factory full of machines and empty of people.

Indian dealers were as lonesome as Indian factory hands. Some failed to sell a single new Indian during the year. But a poor business was better than no job. Somehow, most of them survived by making repairs and selling used motorcycles.

The Dry-Sump Twins

Indian attacked this miserable situation with one of the more important engineering updates in company history. The 1933 Indian twins received the major improvement of dry-sump (circulating) lubrication. In both the old total-loss system and the new circulating system, oil was pumped from the tank to the crankcase by a reciprocating plunger. In the old system the crankcase oil was consumed. In the new circulating system, a sump valve in the bottom of the crankcase scooped up excess oil, which was then returned to the tank by the bottom part of the reciprocating plunger. The new dry-sump system greatly increased oil mileage and minimized the risk of running out of the vital fluid.

Predictably, there were problems with the pump. During 1933 and 1934, Indian tried three different oil-pump-drive worm gears; these worm gears were cut on the front camshaft. Also, different combinations of pumping pistons and sump (suction, or return) valves were used. Finally, after periods when these different combinations of parts resulted in overoiling and underoiling, the design of the dry-sump system stabilized in 1935.

To accommodate the dry-sump pump and a new standard battery ignition, there was a different cam case cover for both battery- and magneto-ignition models. To accommodate the sump valve and the standard battery ignition, new right crankcases were required for battery- and magneto-ignition Chiefs. Both the battery- and magneto-ignition Chiefs dispensed with the compression release, so there was no "relief cam" (compression release) bushing in the right crankcase of either. Battery and magneto-ignition Chiefs also got a left crankcase assembly that no longer incorporated an elbow for the auxiliary oil hand pump tube (there was no hand pump).

The circuit-breaker mechanism was relocated to the cam case cover on the battery-ignition Chiefs. This design dispensed with the expensive intermediate drive gears that had formerly operated the front-mounted circuit breaker. The new drive was from the rear camshaft.

All 1933 cylinder heads and cylinders were black, whereas in 1932 some early production models may have been nickel-plated. The new C-2 Edison Splitdorf magneto had a different appearance. Some late-1933 models may have had 14-millimeter spark plugs instead of 18-millimeter plugs. The exhaust system featured a tubular (not cast) connector to join the front and rear sections and it had two new support clips.

Linking the motor and the transmission was a primary drive gear case that featured an integral generator takeoff drive. Because of the newly shaped generator drive section a different generator belt guard was fitted. A two-piece battery anchor strap assembly was installed.

Prior to 1933, customers could order special plating on individual items. This practice continued in 1933, but a special chromium-plating combination was also offered as a convenience to the factory as well as a cost savings for the customers. The 1933 optional chromium plating combination included the items most frequently requested by customers. The chrome-plated parts in the combination were handlebar (including clip, screw, and cover plate), carburetor air horn, bumper retainer and screw, valve-spring covers, taillight body, exhaust tubes, and "sundry other parts"—a total of 17 or more separate items. Cadmium-plated rims were also part of the chromium-plating package. Indian offered the option throughout the 1930s, although the company did not always list or explain the option in publicity releases.

1934: Chain Primary Drive

For the 1934 season Indian changed the Chief and Scout primary drive from helical gears to a

These are 1933-only sheet-metal tanks. Late-1931 and 1932 tanks had the same shape but the right tank had an oil head-lamp. Beginning in 1932, the accessory speedometer was center-mounted and a cast-iron front saddle connection replaced the former simple rolled-strap iron connection. Because of the automatic dry-sump lubrication, the auxiliary oil hand pump was omitted.

four-row chain. An important factor was the lower cost of chain drive because sprockets, even with multirows, are less costly than helical gears. Another cost factor was the old and sloppy factory tooling that resulted in too much rework on the earlier gear drive. Tolerances weren't as critical on the chain drive, so the worn tooling wasn't a drawback and rework was reduced.

Old-timers mourned the departed helical gears. Riders liked the solid feel of the old gear drive and salesmen liked to brag about the old gear drive for its obvious quality. Still, the switch to chain drive was one of those rare instances in which, for the most part, cheaper was better. Although Indian had to give up the gear-drive bragging rights, the change to chain drive was logical because the less expensive multirow chain in an oil bath would outlast the rest of the motorcycle. Indeed, in about 30,000 miles of Chief riding, your author made only one primary-chain adjustment. This was done

The 1933 quick-detach rear wheel was secured by three long stud bolts and three receiving (locator) pins. This layout was unique to 1933 models. The axle-type drive for the speedometer was first available on 1931 models.

to drive the oil pump at a faster speed. The term "quadruple-thread" means that there were four parallel threads cut into the shaft; see the accompanying photos for clarification. The revised pump assembly was termed the "four-speed pump." This is a term that from time to time has driven Indian restorers nuts. Who could blame restorers for unsuccessfully trying to figure out the "obvious" connection between the four-speed oil pump and the Indian four-speed transmission that came out about that time? Sorry, but there was no connection at all.

In the old oil pump, the single-thread plunger had a 7/16-inch diameter. The new dry-sump pump assembly included a 3/8-inch-diameter quadruple-thread plunger, factory number (FN) 39616, to work with the worm gears of the quadruple-thread "four-speed" camshaft drive. Because of the different plunger diameter, the old and new pump bodies were not interchangeable; the new pump body was listed under a different FN. By products of the four-

after the recommended first 500 miles, and even then, the chain wasn't too slack according to the rider's handbook. As a bonus, chain primary drive also reduced running noise; Indian twins were no longer derided for having built-in police sirens. Enclosing the new chain drive was a new drive case with cover. The housing had a different shape and the cover was embossed with Indian script.

New Right and Left Crankcases

The right and left crankcases of battery- and magneto-ignition models had no transmission mounting studs because the transmission was now bolted to the back of the crankcase. The left crankcase had an added flange (with three screw holes) around the drive shaft support to mount the front of the new primary chain case. During the model year, a running change incorporated a different left crankcase for motor numbers CCD-483 and up. The revised left crankcase "assembly" included the crankcase breather, which had been on the timing-case cover of the early-1934 Chiefs. For Chiefs with motor number CCD-483 and up, the crankcase breather tube was routed from the left crankcase to the oil compartment of the right tank. These resulted in a late-1934-only right tank.

Sorting Out the Dry-Sump Lubrication

Running changes were made to the dry-sump lubrication system. Motor numbers CCD-483 and up had a new front camshaft with the worm drive changed from a single-thread to quadruple-thread

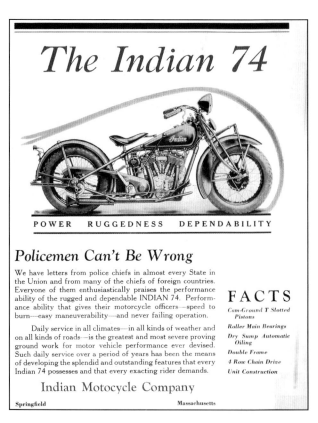

The 1934 Chief was essentially unchanged from the 1933 model. With the easy-handling 101 Scout no longer around, the Chief was again prominently pitched as a cop bike. The Pennsylvania Highway Patrol purchased more than 600 Indians (Chiefs and Scouts) and the Massachusetts state police bought 200 Chiefs.

In 1934 the Chief's primary drive was switched from helical gears to chain and sprockets. The chain drive was cheaper, quieter, and would outlast the motorcycle.

speed oil pump were new factory numbers for the "front cam assembly four-speed" and its subassembly the "front cam shaft four-speed."

Motor numbers CCD-460 through CCD-1344 got a revised sump screen and housing assembly, details are unknown except that it still used a non-spring-loaded disc. Motor numbers CCD-1345 through CCD-1567 switched from a nonspring-loaded disc valve to a single-reed valve (applicable FNs unknown). This change was made to reduce the overoiling experienced with the four-speed oil pump. Motor numbers CCD-1568 and up switched from a single-reed valve to a triple-reed valve. The reed valve installation was discernible from the exterior because of the small reed base plate and mounting screw at the six-o'clock position on the sump-valve base.

Standard cast-iron cylinder heads for the Chief had the spark plug mounted at an angle. All spark plugs were 14 millimeters instead of 18 millimeters; this change was officially announced on the 1934 models but may have applied to late-1933 motorcycles as well. The iron cylinder-fin structure was identical to the 1932–1933 heads. Optional aluminum heads were identically shaped. The one-year-only aluminum heads weren't listed in the parts book but were included in the dealer's (wholesale) price list. New alloy pistons for the Chief had a different oil-control ring and featured a T slot to compensate for thermal expansion.

Other Changes

A longer side stand was provided on 1934 models. On the rear wheel, six studs replaced the earlier combination of three studs and three driving pins.

The "1934 Price List Indian Motocycles" confirms the availability of chrome-plated wheel rims for the 1934 models. Indian had a habit of not listing all options. Because of this, and the fact that the chrome wheel rims option was listed in 1936, 1939, and 1941 price lists, it's safe to conclude that chrome wheel rims were offered every year after 1934.

Indian President E. Paul du Pont's family connections enabled Indian to buy paint cheaply, which resulted in an explosion of color options. The "color war" with Harley-Davidson reached its zenith in 1934, when Indian offered 24 standard one- and two-color options, plus offering the extra-cost option of any nonlisted colors available from DuPont paints. The front safety (crash) guard was first offered in November 1933. This became one of the more popular accessory items.

Better Roads Renew the Transcontinental Game

Transcontinental motorcycle records hadn't been attempted since the 1920s because the factories feared bad publicity. The game was at last renewed in June 1934. C. Randolph Whiting rode a 1930 Chief to a new transcontinental solo record of 122 hours and 49 minutes. He made more than 1,000 miles in one 24-hour period, made 71 miles in one hour, rode 85 miles per hour for 13 minutes, and maintained speeds of 60 to 70 miles per hour for hour after hour. Whiting's run beat Cannon

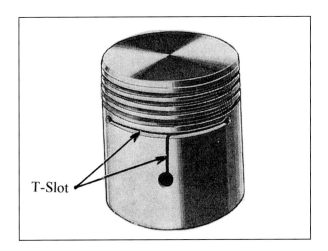

Optional alloy T-slot pistons were new for 1934. The slots compensated for thermal expansion, which was a special problem for side-valve engines because of the heat built up around the exhaust port. Cast-iron "hour glass" pistons were continued until stocks were used up, then replaced by cast-iron T-slot pistons.

When Everybody Played Outdoors

Harold Mathewson ran a small Indian shop in Fresno, California. Small, but efficient. Mathewson outsold the local Harley-Davidson dealer, and not many Indian dealers could make that claim. But times were hard enough that Mathewson supplemented his motorcycle income with a job as the rural delivery agent for the local newspaper, the *Fresno Bee*. Of course, Mathewson insisted that all his delivery riders use Indians.

Club life was important in motorcycling and Mathewson had a clubhouse a few miles outside Fresno. One of his members, Franky Rogers, turned colors and bought a used Harley from the highway department. This, however, wasn't just any Harley-Davidson. The motorcycle had been used by Patrolman Sprouts Elder, who earlier had achieved international fame as a speedway racer. In fact, Elder had practically invented speedway, and decades later is still the subject of much prose by motorcycle journalists of Britain, Australia, and New Zealand. This was an ex-Elder bike because Elder had a horrible crash with it, a crash that finished his motorcycle-riding days forever.

The ex-Elder Harley had special heads, barrels, cams—the works—and had been timed at 106 miles per hour. That was some going for a side-valve Harley Seventy-four with full road equipment. Franky Rogers lost no time in riding it out to the Mathewson clubhouse, and on the way back home that evening he trimmed by a wide margin the club's favorite Indian hotshoe, R. V. Drown. Drown, who rode a new Chief, was despondent.

The next day, Mathewson called the West Coast Indian distributor Hap Alzina. Mathewson had favors due, and he cashed in his chips. Alzina agreed to ship a special Chief motor to Mathewson. This was a way-out Chief engine, with special heads, "Swiss cheese" pistons, special porting in the barrels, drilled connecting rods, and you name it. The special Chief had been timed at over 120 miles per hour on a dry-lake run. Meanwhile, Franky Rogers and the Harley-Davidson shop had been spreading the word about an upcoming match race between a used Harley and a new Indian Chief. At home in his garage Mathewson and a couple of friends secretly swapped the stock Chief engine for the special Chief engine. The special motor was too clean, so the boys gave it a good exterior coating of dirt and oil, making it look like a proper newspaper delivery cycle. The stage was set.

A few days later the club met again and following the usual preliminaries, minutes of the last meeting, old business, new business, and the like, the real business came up. It was about midnight when Franky Rogers on the hot Harley VL and R. V. Drown on the very special Chief, headed for their match race along a 1.5-mile paved stretch alongside a eucalyptus grove. To Mathewson's amazement, several hundred people were on hand, in cars and on motorcycles. Most of them were Harley people who had come to see this embarrassment of the Indian guys. They included a dealer and his entourage who had come from 60 miles away, and this in a day when driving on dirt roads was mainly a 20-mile-per-hour experience. Cars and motorcycles on both sides of the road turned on their lights for the racers. There was a lot of betting, and some reckless types wagered as much as $10, a week's pay, if you had a job.

The two riders rode out ahead for a mile and a half, until the taillights almost disappeared and then could be seen turning around, the two tiny headlights staring back at the crowd. The motors could be heard, even at that distance, as the race began. Then a roar, and then silence again. Somebody had missed a shift. The pair made a U-turn and went back to the starting point. Off

Ball Baker's one-man record in a Stutz car and the official automobile record made with an Essex Six and a team of three drivers. The record set the stage for a series of transcontinental motorcycle record runs in the 1930s.

Whiting's record was also a tribute to improved highways and roads. The previous motorcycle record holder was Paul Remally, who turned the trick in 1923. Remally rode about 129 hours and slept but 8 hours on the whole crossing. Whiting's 1934 riding time was 60 hours and 7 minutes, about half of Remally's.

Spacemen, Art Deco, and Airflows

Movie theaters across the nation were showing the new serialized Flash Gordon adventures. These episodes were guilty of very unspecial effects, with rocket ships exhausting flames as timid as a cigarette lighter and flying Hawkmen who were obviously hanging from wires. But Flash Gordon wore streamlined clothes, flew streamlined rockets, and was as modern as the future. The public liked anything that was either streamlined or modern, and again, it became clear the boys were using a rolling start this time.

With an edge of 15 miles per hour or more, the Chief rider got to the crowd with a 200-yard lead on the Harley rider. The Harley rider was so embarrassed he went flying by and continued home—no stopping for him in the middle of the Indian celebration. The Indian fans in the crowd were honking horns. The Chief victor, R. V. Drown, walked among the fastest of the Harley riders. Although women and children were present, Drown crowed loudly and profanely, challenging the ancestry of all the Harley riders, while pointing out that he had merely removed his newspaper bags in preparation for the outing; and since he had gone to that much trouble, Drown reckoned he should get in a few more fast miles. The Harley riders, of course, couldn't resist a run. The special Chief ran seven more times and won these matchups even more handily. The Milwaukee faithful among the crowd had dispersed long before the last VL was trimmed, but the Springfield fans stayed on.

How could people, some of them not even serious motorcycle fans, get so worked up over an informal race? Americans hadn't yet come under the full spell of indoor entertainment via the radio, let alone television. Air conditioning, too, was a pipe dream. Motorcyclists had the better of it, for there was no better toy than a motorcycle for chasing away the heat of the day. But motorcyclist or not, in the summer time you played outdoors. For fun you met up with real people, and you either played games or you watched other real people play games. At such times you forgot about the troubles of a very troubled era. Motorcyclist or not, you were out in the world and it was exciting.

loved anything that was both. Art deco, an art form emphasizing geometric shapes, graced the walls of new courthouses, post offices, and commercial buildings. Harley-Davidson took a cue, so the 1933 and 1934 Harleys had art deco tank designs. Chrysler sensed the value of visual excitement as well, but overstepped in designing radically different Chrysler and De Soto Airflow automobiles that were so streamlined they failed. Airflows were the exceptions that proved the rule, however. The buzz

Indian used three different worm gears (on the front camshaft) to drive the oil pump during 1933 and 1934. Indian also varied other pump and crankcase breather details in conjunction with these pumps. The worm gears are shown left to right, in the order that they were used. Left, single-speed worm, used on all 1933 and some 1934 twins; center, four-speed worm, used on some 1934 twins; right, two-speed worm, used on some 1934 45-cubic-inch motors.

word of the day stayed in place. The word? "Streamline" and its derivatives "streamlined" and "streamlining." The automobile industry and the motorcycle industry were on the eve of rapidly changing ideas about how much streamlining was enough. Soon, General Motors, Ford, and Chrysler would think nothing of completely changing car bodies at two- and three-year intervals. Indian launched its streamlining trial balloon, the 45-cubic-inch Sport Scout, and its styling was validated.

The first four years of E. Paul du Pont's presidency, 1930 to 1934, had seen Indian almost go under. Arriving at the juncture of bad times and a bad motorcycle, the Chief, Mr. du Pont had fixed the latter problem with major styling and engineering updates. The Chief was now the equal of the Harley-Davidson big twin in the equally important realms of speed and reliability.

Chapter 4

Better Roads Mean Faster Riding
1935–1936

Motorcycle touring benefited by the evolution of roads, vehicle servicing, and tourist accommodations that by 1935 had defined a new motor age. Of improved roads, enough has been said, so I'll merely add that progress in the nation's highways continued without interruption except during the World War II years.

Vehicle servicing started out as help-yourself at the local hardware store where barrels of gasoline were stocked. America's first drive-in gas station opened in late 1913. By 1935, uniformed service-station attendants rushed to provide full service to every car in tens of thousands of filling stations

This late-1935 Chief has the Y motor, optional for 1935–1936 and standard for 1937–1938. Two major changes for 1936 were standard distributor ignition and positive lubrication of the valve guides through the two small T fittings (choosing change, late-1935). Unfortunately, the T fittings leaked.

Larger quick-action bayonet filler caps were featured in the 1930s. Chrome-plated handlebars and instrument panel were extra-cost options. Indian offered a chrome-plating package throughout the 1930s, which included other parts such as headlight, taillight bracket, and wheel rims. In 1936, the package included "over fifteen items," which were not specified.

For 1935, streamlined fenders and optional plain, Arrow, or V tank panels (shown here) were fitted. The optional Y motor had larger fins, aluminum heads, and nickel-plated cylinders. This motorcycle was restored by Bollenbach Engineering.

across the continent. Motorcyclists continued to do their own servicing, but benefited from the full-service philosophy in other ways. No longer did they have to look for a roadside bush when nature called. They used the clean rest rooms that were proudly advertised by the service stations. Gone too were the old 1920s "blue books" of detailed travel directions. In their place, oil companies handed out free, detailed road maps. The maps worked because most of the better roads were by this time numbered on the maps and marked on the roadside signs. The covers and inserts of these maps were lavishly illustrated by top-rate artists, projecting images of open-road adventure. The maps folded up to fit in your pocket. If you damaged the map or lost it, you just picked up another free map at the next gas stop.

Tourist accommodations had also evolved. Prior to 1920, tourists had two opposite alternatives, downtown hotels or camping out. Hotels were

relatively expensive and formal, with uniformed doormen, waiters, and bellboys forever extending their hands for tips. Traditional hotels were fine for an affluent minority of car travelers, but universally unacceptable for motorcyclists who were generally not of the "carriage" set and, even if affluent, were not inclined to the formalities. There was also the matter of class consciousness; bikers were viewed with condescension, and, in some cases, denied accommodations.

At the other extreme of pre-1920s choices was camping out. No KOAs here. You just looked for a

The 1935 front fork had two rebound leaves on the top. The correct handgrips were also the same as the 1922–1927 handgrips. The jump seat was flipped forward for solo riding. This primary-drive cover (for chain drive) debuted on 1934 models. Indian script was used on all 1934–1939 covers and a few 1940 covers.

good spot and stopped. This worked better for car travelers than for motorcyclists because tents occupied a relatively larger part of the luggage capacity on motorcycles.

In the 1920s, reports John Margolies in his book *Home Away From Home*, a few cities began to open free municipal campgrounds for motorists. Accommodations varied from nothing but tent space to permanent tents erected over board frames, to frame or log-cabin structures. In 1920, 300 cities provided these free tourist parks; by 1923, 2,000 cities did so. The commercial motel industry was thus inspired. Commercial roadside cabins numbered 1,000 locales in 1920 and 2,000 by 1926. Many service stations got into the motel business by hastily erecting primitive cabins. By 1935, the better motels cost $1 a night and featured restaurants. Two bucks bought you more space and more furniture. Fifty cents bought you a more Spartan room at a place without a restaurant. Margolies reported that 9,848 motels were in business in 1935; this grew 39 percent to 13,521 in 1939; and pre-World War II motel registrations totaled 225 million.

All of this worked to the advantage of touring riders, primarily those who rode Indian Chiefs or

The right and left filler caps of the 1935 tanks were spaced farther from each other, creating the illusion that the tanks were wider. On the left tank, the filler cap no longer had an integral injector (priming syringe). The smaller saddle was for the rider, while a passenger uses the main saddle, a riding style referred to as "short coupled." When riding alone, the rider flipped the smaller saddle forward.

Left & Above
For 1935–1938 Chiefs, Indian used these unusual cylinder heads, which were sometimes termed "Ricardo" heads (photo at left). Earlier and later heads had neither the cutout "trench" between the area over the valves and the area over the cylinder bore nor the tucked-in outline around the valve and bore areas (head at right above). The Ricardo or "trench" heads maximized midrange torque but fell out of favor because they produced less top speed. Mark Dooley's DG Performance Specialties builds these beautiful reproduction heads as well as other 1930s and 1940s parts. Mark Dooley

Harley-Davidson big twins. Motorcycle touring was no longer a feat of stamina, so that more and more long-distance riding was done by couples. Harley-Davidson's introduction of the buddy seat in late 1933, and Indian's copy of it soon thereafter, blended right in with better roads, better service, and better lodging to bring a new civility to motorcycle touring.

1935: New Styling

The Chief joined the styling trend launched by the mid-1934 Sport Scout by having an Indian-head decal on each tank side. For the standard tank panels, profiles continued to be outlined in narrow double-line striping, each stripe being about 3/64 inch wide. There were two new tank trim choices, the Arrow panel and the V panel. Streamlined front and rear fenders were fitted; these were the same in appearance as those of the mid-1934 Sport Scout except that the front fender on the Chief had a deeper valance. This fender was also fitted to the 1935 Scout and Four. The new fenders and other changes caused the Chief's dry weight to grow from 445 to 481 pounds. On Chiefs with single-color finishes, the center section (crown) of each fender was bounded by double striping, each stripe about 3/64 inch wide. On Chiefs with two-color finishes, these fender centers were bounded by a single stripe about 3/16 inch wide.

An optional "oversize" 4.50x18-inch front tire was available. The front fork had two rebound leaves added to the top, a total of 10 leaves. On the left tank, the filler cap no longer had an integral injector (priming syringe).

The carburetor air horn was shaped like a tear drop or "arrow"; formerly it was round. On the exhaust system two tabs were welded to the front exhaust tube, which, after curving back, continued horizontally and hence parallel to the lower right frame tube. The two tabs accommodated two P-shaped mounting clips on the lower frame tube. One of these clips was mounted slightly ahead of the rear exhaust pipe and the other clip was slightly behind the kickstarter.

Transmission functional changes also impacted the appearance. Transmission options were a three-speed-and-reverse gearbox and a four-speed gearbox. The optional gearboxes featured taller and differently shaped shift towers.

The battery filler inlets were exposed in normal running configuration; in other words, the rider didn't have to remove a battery top to service the battery. The toolbox was taller and narrower, and it had a full-length door hinge. The muffler had the cutout on the rear instead of the front and had hemispherical sections at the front and the rear. As noted earlier, the rear fender was restyled—the same in general appearance as the 1934 Sport Scout rear fender. Due to the different fender surface contours, a different taillight was fitted.

An optional "oversize" 4.50x18-inch rear tire was also available. The rear wheel was quickly detachable via six studs and six tapered-head lug nuts. A new rear-wheel hub shell had a larger diameter between the flanges and had one flange with six countersunk holes to accept the six tapered lug nuts. There was no Alemite grease fitting on the rear hub.

New Motors with "Trench" Heads

Two styles of Chief motors were available: the standard motor and the Y motor. The standard motors had regular-sized nickel-plated cylinders and nickel-plated iron heads.

All of the standard motors were termed B motors, a bit of a gimmick, as the B designation had previously been used only for extra-fast motors built off-line using special assembly factors. It would not have been possible to mass-produce the real B motors, but the advertising department felt like elevating the status of the standard motors due to the arrival of the new Y series. The regular-sized optional aluminum heads (non-Y) offered in 1934 were discontinued because of the new optional Y motors.

The Y motors weren't special jobs either but were instead improved mass-produced engines. The Y motors were listed in the 1935 parts book, although not in the 1935 sales literature. This suggests the Y motor option was a running change. The Y motors had larger nickel-plated cylinders and larger aluminum (unplated) cylinder heads. The Y cylinder assemblies incorporated different valve guides. All Chief Y heads had cooling fins angled into the air stream instead of the earlier fore-and-aft configuration. Also the cylinder heads had no priming-cup boss. Chief Y motor cylinders had 13 cooling fins instead of 12, two minifins around the exhaust port, larger fins throughout, and were nickel-plated.

Several changes applied to both the B and Y motors. During the model year, the carburetor finish was changed to black. For the connecting rods, four aluminum roller retainers replaced the earlier steel retainers (this eventually proved a mistake, and in 1939 the old retainers were reinstated). Four-piece center-clipped clamshell valve covers paved the way for next year's oil lines to the valve guides, evidence that the engineering department was already experimenting in this area. The

In June 1935, brothers C. Randolph and Roger Whiting were smiling after setting a transcontinental record of 4 days, 20 hours, and 36 minutes while riding double. Improved roads were a big factor in the unprecedented and unrepeated record. Floyd Clymer collection

larger-diameter, cadmium-plated covers mated with the new valve guides and new pushrod guides. Because of the revised pushrod guides, the right crankcase assemblies (on both battery and magneto models) got new factory numbers. On the right crankcase, the sump-valve base no longer had a screwed-on reed-valve base.

The Chief oil pump was still a so-called four-speed (one speed but four separate worm threads). Also, the new pump still used a 3/8-inch plunger, as evidenced by the fact that the new pump used the same body as the previous pump. The plunger, however, was given a new factory number, so it differed somehow.

For both B and Y motors, Indian claimed thicker stems for the inlet and exhaust valves. The new and old valves were interchangeable, so by "thicker"

stems Indian referred to the shape near the valve head. The valve shape was described as "new" and "tulip." The valves were closed by heavier inlet- and exhaust-valve springs. Operating the valves were the new standard high-lift cams; optional were the lower-lift cam profiles of 1934.

All Y motors used the new so-called Ricardo cylinder heads (later they were nicknamed "trench" heads). Incidentally, Harley-Davidson was paying royalties to England's Sir Harry Ricardo for the design of similar Harley heads. But in the case of Indian the term "Ricardo" is informal because there's no evidence that these Indian heads were designed outside the Wigwam. The Ricardo heads featured a sort of inverted-V roof similar to that of a house. Commonly thought to be low-compression heads due to the additional cylinder head height above the piston, the Ricardo heads actually had the same compression ratio as the earlier heads, about 5.:1 in the case of the Chief.

Keeping the same compression ratio on the Y motor Ricardo heads was achieved by tucking in the head volume around the lower edges where the head mated with the cylinder and by gradually letting the combustion chamber roof climb to its peak. The resulting configuration was sometimes termed a heart-shaped combustion chamber. The combustion chamber might be more accurately described as a Mickey Mouse shape when viewed from above, with the ears representing the valve areas and the face representing the piston area.

New cam profiles in combination with the Ricardo heads produced significantly higher low- and midrange torque. Moreover, the improved breathing characteristics and the new four-speed transmission were an integrated design effort so that all features worked together with optimum results. The four-speed transmission was designed primarily for sidecar use, so there was a very low first gear to get all the metal moving. Second gear was spaced close to low gear, then there was a big gap between second and third gear, and fourth gear was spaced close to third gear. Proper rider technique was to spend a minimum of time in low gear to get the Chief up to only about one-half of maximum revolutions, and then shift to second gear, where the Ricardo heads pulled tractor-fashion, despite the drop-off in engine revolutions. The Chief was brought to nearly full engine speed in second gear before making the big jump up to third gear. The closely spaced third and fourth gears were ideal for sidecar highway cruising because shifting between the two gears was smooth. Dropping down to third gear increased the engine speed just enough to allow the Ricardo heads and new cams to maintain sidecar cruising speed on most hills. Only a few four-speed transmissions have survived, and most run noisily in third gear because of previous sidecar use. The gear ratios aren't practical for solo (single-track) use because there's no benefit from the close pairing of low and second gears.

The Indian Engineering Staff

Thanks to a trip report by Harley-Davidson junior executive William H. Davidson, we get an insight into how Indian ran its engineering efforts. Davidson, with Milwaukee's operations in mind, was surprised that so few people could do so much

Club uniforms and disciplined formation road riding were popular in the 1930s. Gals favored white outfits. This woman's riding breeches, loose above the knees and tight below the knees, were called "jodhpurs." Butch Baer collection

work in Springfield. The Indian engineering department consisted of only six men, including a draftsman. The experimental room was manned by just three people.

Trying for Long-Distance Records

Since 1933 the American Motorcycle Association (AMA) had sustained Class C competition for stock motorcycles and unsponsored riders. Class C was in response to the falloff in popularity of Class A (which featured factory-sponsored teams and special motorcycles) and Class B competition (which allowed amateur riders to use modified motorcycles). Interest in Class C stock racing and hill climbing grew steadily, so that by 1935 the Indian and Harley-Davidson factories were highlighting Class C victories with the appealing claim that the winners rode same-as-you-can-buy motorcycles.

In May 1935, Indian decided to try for some Class C records, using the Chief and the Sport Scout for their respective Class C categories of 74-cubic-inch (1,200-cc) side-valve and 45-cubic-inch (750-cc) side-valve. The site chosen was the Muroc

Dry Lake, about 90 miles north of Los Angeles in the Mojave Desert, and the manager of the effort was West Coast distributor Hap Alzina. The riders were a well-known bunch. Kenny Scholfield had shown impressive skills on the short-track (speedway) circuit. Van De Mark had speed-trial experience as a Four specialist. Short-track star Bo Lisman had celebrity status. Al Laurer was a competition all-arounder and the Indian dealer for Sacramento. Most illustrious was former Indian and Harley factory rider Fred Ludlow, now a Pasadena motorcycle cop. Back in the 1920s Ludlow had won five national championship titles in one day!

The May schedule was interesting because the participants knew about the strong winds that typically blew across Muroc in May and lasted into the summer. The reason for the May schedule was to take advantage of the brick-hard dry-lake surface that came after the spring rains had stopped. The rainwater had baked into the ground.

On hand for these scheduled round-the-clock speed runs was *The Motorcyclist* editor Chet Billings. The speed runs started at 6:00 A.M. The Chief maintained an 80-mile-per-hour pace and the Sport Scout a 75-mile-per-hour pace. The Chief logged its first 100 miles in 1 hour, 17 minutes, and 48 seconds. This broke the old board-track record for 100 miles set back in 1922 by Wells Bennett on a Henderson Four. The Chief completed 200 miles in 2 hours, 36 minutes, and 14 seconds, another record. This was an average of about 77 miles per hour.

Unfortunately, the Chief began to splatter from overheating, so it was brought into the pits. No problem could be found, so it returned to the circular course only to again overheat in a couple of laps. After another pit stop and a rider change, it overheated again. On the next pit stop the problem was diagnosed—blocked flow in the oil supply line. Then, another record was set, this one for 300 miles, and the time was 3 hours, 54 minutes, and 46 seconds, an average of about 76 1/2 miles per hour. A new 400-mile mark was set at 5 hours, 33 minutes, and 36 seconds, beating the old Henderson mark by nearly 13 minutes. At this point, a glamorous 500-mile record was still possible despite the several pit stops. But with only seven laps to go, the Chief came in for an ailment mysteriously undisclosed by editor Billings. The Chief was in the pits 1 hour and 3 minutes.

The battle was renewed, for the magical 1,000-mile record was still attainable, as was the 24-hour record. That was because of the Chief's proven 80-mile-per-hour cruising speed, as compared to Bennett's old Henderson pace of 65 miles per hour. But

at 9:45:47, the Chief again limped into the pits, after 15 hours and nearly 46 minutes. The Chief had logged 1,050 miles, but the 1,000-mile record had been barely missed. Incidentally, the 100-, 200-, 300-, and 400-mile records were more than Class C records; they were absolute records. The Sport Scout gave up the ghost several hours before the Chief, again with undisclosed ailments. Friendly editor Billings wrote an interesting blow-by-blow story of the Muroc Dry Lake runs. Billings called the effort a successful mechanical test conducted for the Indian engineering program, thus masking the disappointment of having fallen short of the glamorous marks for 500 and 1,000 miles, and potentially, for 24 hours.

Odd Long-Distance Record

In June 1935 a Chief was ridden to an unprecedented and unrepeated record. Brothers C. Randolph and Roger Whiting set a transcontinental record of 4 days, 20 hours, and 36 minutes, while riding double. (Randolph, as noted earlier, also set a transcontinental solo record in 1934.)

Preparations for the coast-to-coast run included practice spins totaling 2,647 miles, and trials on six engines, which each had their turn for burning up, blowing up, or wearing out. The Whiting brothers were amateur motorcyclists, and they weren't wealthy. These facts hinted that the Indian factory was behind the transcontinental effort.

From Randolph Whiting's retrospective article in the April 1940 issue of *Mechanics Illustrated*, only a little reading between the lines is needed to confirm the suspicion of Indian factory support. Randolph said, "I had virtually designed a new engine for this trip." Next, he explained his "suping" ideas as well as the features of the Y motor: "The flywheel had been lightened [Whiting's modification] to get extra acceleration. Larger manifolding and carburetor added to the power. An improved dry sump oiling system had been devised. The final test motor, with higher compression, larger valves, higher lift cams, and an extremely hot high-tension magneto, had been adopted by the manufacturers." Then came the clincher: "Our record cycle was a 'pilot' model, preceding regular production, but it was a stock job, right off the assembly line."

Randolph also described the start of the record run: " . . . [W]e started the transcontinental run, at exactly one minute past midnight, May 27, 1935, and we knew we had a 'hot' engine, capable of high cruising speeds. Our equipment was packed in the saddlebags, our night goggles snapped tight over our eyes, and to the accompaniment of family good-byes and the official wave of William Heisermann of the American Motorcycle Association, we shoved off from the New York side of the Holland Tunnel. I twisted the throttle, the 'Y' motor roared, and we raced through the white-tiled tunnel, dead in the center of the lane police had cleared for us six minutes before. Before we were halfway under the Hudson River the speedometer needle was flicking 85."

In the first 100 miles of riding the brothers twice put the Chief on full throttle to easily outrun chasing motorcycle cops, who, evidently, were on Harleys. Their closest cop chaser was a police car, which the boys outran by letting the Chief run a steady 80 miles per hour. In Pennsylvania, at three in the morning, they had a blowout while cruising at 70 miles per hour; but they were rolling again in only 7 minutes—they claimed. "We drove for nearly twenty-four hours after that with hardly a stop, making some of the best time of the trip, although we had expected slower going," Randolph continued. Incidentally, the brothers alternated the handlebar and passenger-seat duties at two-hour intervals. As a precaution, the passenger, who was expected to either rest or sleep, had a safety belt around him and fixed to the motorcycle.

Challenging weather injected a bit more drama into the ride: ". . . [T]he engine was still clicking beautifully, despite our excessive cruising speeds, when we really hit trouble in Iowa. With a scornful disregard for transcontinental cyclists, storms had hit the state, and road after road was flooded. . . . We hit more floods in Nebraska, until we were steering by the telephone poles alongside the inundated highway, with water washing our floorboards.

"Once we zoomed over a small hill and headed straight for a 'dip'—a stream running across the road," Randolph continued. "The warning sign was down and we hit a hundred-foot stretch of mud and water at a clip of nearly sixty miles an hour." After slowing down in the muck and some awkward leg paddling, the boys spilled. In the dark, the Chief fell completely out of sight beneath the slime, and the brothers had to probe for it with a pole.

After finding the bike and pulling it upright, the mud-caked Chief proved difficult to start, but "[f]inally the engine ran again, while I praised the waterproofing job done on the ignition system, and we splattered our way to the next town and a garage with air pressure for cleaning, hot water, and millions of paper towels."

In Utah at two in the morning, the boys were run off the road by a jalopy full of singing cowboys. But cowboys weren't as dangerous as their cows, ac-

For 1936, the onion-shaped gearshift knob replaces the ball knob. This brown example was a period accessory; standard knobs were black. On the front fork was another accessory, the felt-lined, leather-covered "spring oiler." Oiling was through the hole exposed by unthreading the brass cap.

cording to Randolph: "It wasn't until we reached Salt Lake City that we were out of the flood area with its detours and delays. Then all we had to worry about were mountains, rain, snow . . . and cowboys. . . . One cowboy, with the best of intentions, succeeded in herding a hundred head of cattle right across our road. We were able to decelerate to sixty, before we had to start weaving in and out. Once we grazed a cow, bouncing the cycle halfway across the road . . . but we roared on safely.

" . . . Once, in broad daylight, I was dozing on the rear seat when I felt the cycle lurch. I was too tired to open my eyes even when the lurch was repeated. Then we began to bounce. I looked up

The Arrow tank panel, optional for 1935–1939, was less popular than the V tank panel shown previously. The 1936 Indian sales literature listed Indian Red as standard but added, "A variety of other color combinations optional. Special colors at extra cost." Throughout the 1930s, Indian continued the any-color option.

sleepily, to stare straight ahead at a tree that seemingly was rushing at us at fifty miles an hour. Roger had gone to sleep at the handlebars.

". . . I lurched to the left, forcing the cycle to turn, and as my brother woke up enough to resume steering we glanced off the tree and skidded to a stop—not a spill—a hundred yards out in a field. . . .

"The ceaseless grind of two hours driving, two hours resting on the tandem wore us down about fifteen pounds apiece. We had a total of five flats to break the monotony and eat up precious time, but even so, after we stopped for the second and last night in Cheyenne I checked the log at breakfast time to discover we had an average of 58 miles an hour to our credit—including all the stops. . . . We shoved off, set for an all-night run through Utah and Nevada.

"It was just past noon the next day when we crossed into California on the last, hot run of our trip. I was singing figurative hymns of praise to the larger cooling fins on the cylinders and counting the hours on my fingers to see what would happen to the record if all went well. We must have been losing track of our mileage at

4:36 that afternoon, because we were figuring on another hour's run to Los Angeles."

The Whitings didn't expect the Los Angeles city limits to be so far out in the country, so their record run ended abruptly at a 75 mile-per-hour clip when they rode past a group of flag-waving men. Randolph described the finish: "Floyd Clymer, an old-time [Pikes] Peak record holder, half a dozen cyclists, and a couple of policemen had clocked us into the city limits of Los Angeles just 4 days, 20 hours, and 36 minutes after we started. We'd broken my own record by six hours.

". . . that transcontinental jaunt was just a vacation for both of us. Motorcycling is the kind of sport that gets you places and gets you back, with as many thrills as you want. Airplanes go faster . . . but few amateur pilots can make low-cost transcontinental trips."

In a public relations "letter" written to the Indian Motocycle Company, Randolph Whiting said: "The Indian Y motored job which we used in establishing a new transcontinental record . . . is without doubt the finest road holding motorcycle that I

Shown on this 1936 rig is one of the two-color options that were used to good effect on sidecars as well as motorcycles during the 1930s. Typically, the darker color was used for the outlying surfaces and the lighter color for the center surfaces, but for $5 extra these would be painted in reverse, as on this example.

have ever ridden. . . . We averaged 48 miles per gallon of gasoline, 191 miles per quart of oil which is exceptionally good considering the high speed that we reached many times. We cruised mile after mile on long stretches at 70 miles an hour and reached a top speed several times of 87 miles an hour with the two of us riding straight up. The four speed transmission is ideal for long and fast trips and the dry sump system worked to perfection. . . . As to mechanical trouble, we had none and did not even change a set of spark plugs. The machine used was

my own personal mount which I purchased and is stock in every respect even to long handlebars and the air cleaning screen in the carburetor. . . . It handles beautifully, is a bear for power, it is a pleasure to ride it because of its wonderful roadability at any speed."

In the accompanying advertisement, the Indian Motocycle Company bragged that since 1911 Indian had held the transcontinental motorcycle record longer than all other makes combined.

Indian Leadership

Across the board, the 1935 Indian models compared favorably against Harley-Davidson's line-up. Springfield offered a four-cylinder model and a 30.50-cubic-inch low-cost twin without Milwaukee opposition. The 45-cubic-inch Sport Scout and the 74-cubic-inch Chief clearly had more speed than their Harley rivals, thanks to improved porting and Ricardo heads. Springfield's 45-cubic-inch and 74-cubic-inch twins matched the sealed oil-bath primary drives against the Harleys' spray and drip layout. Springfield also was unopposed in offering the options of a four-speed transmission and magneto ignition. But Indian's clear edge was for only this one year, as will be seen.

1936: Y Motor Hullabaloo, Distributor Ignition, Valve Guide Lubrication

Sharing the 1936 models' headlines was the new standard battery-powered distributor ignition system for the twins, which replaced the wasted-spark setup of 1932–1934. The vertically mounted distributor was driven from the rear-cylinder camshaft through a right-angle drive mounted to the cam case cover. A new coil was installed in the customary position in front of the engine, using the integral magneto/coil platform of the left crankcase. There were three distributor wires, one from the coil and one to each spark plug. These three wires were gathered in a nickel-plated routing tube that was clamped to the lower frame tube beneath the tanks.

Elmer Lower restored this rig for his personal use. The 1935–1939 sidecars have the streamlined fenders but the same body as used from 1922 through 1934.

The tandem seat and footrest package had been available on Chiefs since 1922. The tandem seat gradually fell out of favor during the 1930s because of the more popular two-passenger buddy seat.

Today, we occasionally see 1936-and-later Chiefs that have been converted to use the Harley-style double-spark ignition system, also called the wasted-spark system. This conversion is a misguided attempt at improvement. From the introduction of distributor ignition as standard for 1936 until the last 1953 Chief was built, Indian service literature conspicuously omits any discussion of distributor problems. Speaking from personal experience, about 30,000 miles of Chief riding failed to present a single problem with this system.

The cam case cover castings for battery- and magneto-ignition models were identical, so the factory could fine-tune the production balance between these two models near the final assembly process, and reduce the risks of shortages and overages. The cam case cover for magneto-ignition models had the same large hole through which the distributor drive takeoff spun on the battery-ignition Chief. This functionally unnecessary hole was covered by a camshaft cover plate. Also new to the magneto-ignition cam case cover were the front and rear camshaft bushings, the same as in the battery-ignition Chief.

As in 1935, motor numbers CCF-101 through

CCF-1371 had the crankcase breather on the left crankcase. Motor number CCF-1372 and later had the crankcase breather relocated on the cam case cover, but there was no change in the factory number for these later covers.

During the late 1920s and early 1930s Roland "Rollie" Free established a reputation for hopping up Indians. Free was able to speed up 45-cubic-inch (750-cc) Scouts and Sport Scouts so much that they routinely outran 74-cubic-inch (1,200-cc) and larger Harley-Davidson big twins. Free had also for a time been a traveling sales rep for the Indian factory, so he had double credibility when he wrote an impassioned letter to the Indian engineering department. Free related that although he could make Indians run fast, he couldn't keep them running extra fast for very long. The problem was the lack of positive lubrication of the valve guides, a chore that the factory left up to simple crankcase pressure working its way up into the guides. Free called this the "Indian run in rust" system and explained that the rapid valve-guide wear soon caused valves to bounce around and land askew on the valve seats and to wobble around on the seats. So a super Indian stayed super only for a few hundred miles.

For 1936, Indian had an answer to Free's complaint. New T oil lines fed the valve guides. Crankcase pressure still provided the oomph for the oil, but at least the oil was targeted directly through ample tubing to the guides instead of having to climb all the way uphill through the tight spaces between the valves and the guides. The new, four-piece bright nickel-plated "clamshell" clip-on valve spring covers had holes to admit the oil lines. These replaced the 1935-only cadmium-plated clip-on covers that didn't have the oil holes.

Right crankcase assemblies for both battery- and magneto-ignition models were drilled to mount the T oil line that emerged alongside each cylinder, so the right crankcases got a new factory number. Both styles of right crankcases had new front and rear cam bushings to work with new front and rear camshafts.

The 1936 crankshaft was given a new FN, but there were no changes to the connecting rods and flywheels, so the details of the crankshaft change are unknown. A new left crankcase assembly was used because of a different bearing housing (previously termed driving-shaft housing). The bearing housing worked with the revised crankshaft.

Motors CCF-101 through CCF-1371 still had the crankcase-breather tube mounted to the left crankcase and routed to the oil tank. Motors CCF-

L. C. SMITH
Coast-to-Coast Solo Sidecar Record

In September 1936, L. C. "Smittie" Smith rode this Chief and sidecar combination coast to coast in the record time of 3 days, 14 hours, and 55 minutes. The record was unique because Smith didn't have a partner to share the riding.

1372 and later had the crankcase breather relocated to the cam case cover, the left crankcase-breather hole plugged with a breather-hole screw, and the breather tube was routed to the rear chain instead of the oil tank.

The alloy T-slot pistons used on the Y motors were extensively modified with a thickened head, different beveling of the head edges, reinforced piston-pin bosses, and ribbed inside edges. A Y motor notched piston ring was 1/8-inch thick, instead of 3/32-inch thick, and had less wall tension. The notch was also called a "corner groove." This "piston ring" replaced the 1935 "compression ring." There were no changes to the cast-iron pistons of the standard motor, nor to the rings.

A new front camshaft applied to both battery- and magneto-ignition Chiefs. The shaft had a different worm thread design (details unknown) to work with a different oil-pump plunger that pumped more oil. The battery-ignition Chief got a new rear camshaft in order to mate with the distributor drive unit. The magneto-ignition rear camshaft was renumbered, but the details are unknown.

The 1936 dry-sump pump assembly was given a new FN because of the higher-output plunger. The same oil-pump body was used, so the plunger differed in its thread design rather than in its diameter.

The prototype 1936 Chief used in the sales literature had the same frame as before; however, the production frame had a different, more "solid" look in the steering-head area, and the front down tubes merged at their upper end into a heavier forging. A new ignition switch was marked "P OFF I L H" instead of "PARK OFF IGN BRT DIM."

Half-twist "bayonet" tank filler caps were fitted. Chiefs with motor-number CCF-101 through CCF-1371 had the oil compartment of the right tank accepting the crankcase breather tube from the left crankcase. Later Chiefs had that tank opening plugged, and the crankcase breather was routed from the cam case cover to the rear chain. The rider who looked down at the tanks saw a new gearshift lever. On the operating end was an onion-shaped knob to grasp instead of the former spherical knob. From the right side of the motorcycle, the one-year-only shift lever also looked different because it exited the transmission tower with a simple bend. In other words, the 1936 shift lever had a male fitting. (On pre-1936 models the shift lever had a female fitting: The lower end had a cylindrical shape that accepted the transmission bell-crank-lever shaft.)

For the first time, a stoplight switch was provided as standard equipment. The switch had a large cadmium-plated base. To accommodate the standard-equipment stoplight switch, a boss was added to the frame on the lower right, slightly behind the kickstarter. A new streamlined taillight was mounted on a rubber block that was flush with the rear fender. The taillight lens had a spherical shape, and a lens pattern that was used on 1936 and, possibly, 1937 models. The lens had a starburst pattern and was very dark red over its main area. An amber upper area directed light to the license plate.

Indian Loses Technical Leadership

The year 1936 saw Harley-Davidson introduce its dramatically good-looking and technically up-to-the-minute 61-cubic-inch (1,000-cc) overhead-valve big twin, then called the "Sixty-one," and later to achieve enduring fame with the nickname "Knucklehead." The Harley's overhead-valve engine produced more power per cubic inch and permitted higher engine speeds, while adding the promise of significant future power growth. For the first time, Indian trailed Harley-Davidson in technology.

Harley's leadership wasn't confined to the overhead-valve layout. Although in recent years du Pont had insisted on major improvements to the Chief, the updates didn't extend to a modern constant-mesh transmission. Among the improvements introduced on Harley-Davidson's Knucklehead was a four-speed constant-mesh transmission. Indian had been warned earlier.

Here's one of Indian's bigger mistakes. The tiny engineering and experimental departments devoted the bulk of their time to this "upside-down" 1936 Four, so named for the reversal of its valve configuration—inlets on the side, exhausts on the top. These Fours were a tremendous sales flop at a critical time.

Since 1933 the Harley-Davidson three-wheeled 45-cubic-inch Servi-Car had had a constant-mesh gearbox, and the 45-cubic-inch two-wheelers got the constant-mesh box in the 1935 line-up.

Harley-Davidson's constant-mesh transmission was a major improvement over the old sliding-gear transmission used previously by both companies. In the constant-mesh transmission, major shock loads on the gear teeth were eliminated because the gear teeth were always engaged. Shifting was accomplished by moving centrally located dogs (Harley-Davidson called them clutches) into mating orifices at the gears' centers. These dogs were bigger than gear teeth, so big that the dogs were indestructible. The dogs got rounded edges from the slam-bang shifting action, but that didn't matter because the dogs' sole purpose was to change gears.

In contrast, in the sliding-gear transmission the gears were moved along shafts in order to shift to a different gear ratio (i.e., low, second, high). Shifting motion was accomplished by the gear teeth, tooth to tooth, so the meshing and unmeshing of teeth produced rounded corners and extra wear over a considerable portion of the gear-teeth surfaces. In effect, as the miles accumulated on the sliding-gear transmissions, the gears' surface-to-surface contact was constantly reduced, causing increased pressure

on the portion of the teeth contact areas that were still carrying the load under power. In other words, the more the gear teeth wore, the faster they wore. Not only that, but the tooth-to-tooth shifting action was likely to produce a broken tooth or two under abusive use.

Harley-Davidson followed up by incorporating the constant-mesh transmission in its side-valve big twins for the 1937 season. From then on, Indian was deficient in the major areas of big-twin engine and transmission design.

Another Unusual Chief Long-Distance Record

In September, L. C. "Smittie" Smith rode a Chief-and-sidecar combination to a transcontinental sidecar record of 3 days, 14 hours, and 55 minutes. This was the only time a sidecar outfit was ever ridden to a record without a backup rider/passenger to share the duties. Here is *The Motorcyclist* magazine's account, which appeared in the October 1936 issue:

"One of the oddest of transcontinental stories was in the making during the month of September. It is a story of calm, cool record breaking, enacted by one who in as matter-of-fact a manner collected the honors of Class C champion for 1932–33 in District No. 4; came through the Class A sidecar champ at

Here's what made the 1936 Four such a costly error. This is the 1936 Harley-Davidson 61-cubic-inch overhead-valve twin, officially termed the Model E (low-compression) or Model EL (high-compression). In Harley lingo of the era, this was the "Sixty-one OHV," but later it was nicknamed the "Knucklehead." The bottom line: Milwaukee launched one of its best in parallel with one of Springfield's worst, the 1936 Four. What if Indian had made a 1936 overhead-valve big twin instead of the upside-down Four? Copyright Harley-Davidson Michigan, Inc.

the Jack Pines in 1934; and garnered second place for Class C honors in District No. 4 in 1935. In a breath, L. C. Smith of New York City, riding an Indian Chief with an Indian sidecar, holds a new record for crossing this country in 86 hours and 55 minutes.

"At almost exactly the same time of the month last year, Earl and Dorothy Robinson made the run, also from West to East, and established the time of 89 hours and 58 minutes.

"Smittie' varied the procedure and made the trip alone, carrying only his baggage in his sidehack.

"It may be wondered why 'Smittie,' living in New York, made a record running from the West Coast to the East Coast. Why didn't he take a shot at it both ways? To be honest about it, he did. In fact, he came so close to breaking the record twice instead of once that his experience is worth retelling.

"Leaving the Holland Tunnel he blotted out the good luck wishes of starter Connolly with a blast from his exhaust. Being one of those individuals in this world who run to a certain amount of 'beef,' 'Smittie' chuckled when he thought of how his competitors before him had worried about food. He knew he could live off his own store of strength for a long time, the whole distance if necessary. According to his lights there was no need for a lot of stopping. All he had to do was to keep his mount supplied with fuel and sit there and ride. And 'Smittie' had worked out his own little idea of how to rapidly refuel.

"Halfway across the United States he reached into the sidecar and pulled out a small paper sack. In it was his lunch. It could have been stuffed into the side pocket of any coat. As he rode he munched on something. That too was 'Smittie's' secret. Then he calmly rode on to Salt Lake. This was without sleep.

"Now while the hero could apparently go like a camel without much to eat or drink, he did lack a store of rest on which he could draw as he rode. When he stopped to fill up at Salt Lake he was pretty tired. In fact, he was so tired his thinking powers were numbed a little. While they refueled his motor he reviewed his figures. Unlike his brother transcontinentalists he had not bothered with a schedule. And depending entirely on memory was his downfall. As that memory grew ragged from the steady grind he confused the solo record with the sidecar.

"Still ahead of the sidecar record when he left Salt Lake, 'Smittie' had a dealer wire to Los Angeles that he was coming. Scouts were sent to help him find his way over the highways from the state line to the end of his journey. The outmost scout and 'Smittie' were rapidly approaching each other within the southern limits of the 700-mile grind toward the finish. They were within 125 miles of each other. Then 'Smittie' roused from his lethargy and did a little figuring. Instead of figuring 89 hours he figured 78 hours. All at once it dawned on him that he couldn't make it within 78 hours. 'Huh,' he thought to himself, 'I lost.' Well, that was that. So he found a place to stop and took himself a nap that lasted all day. Scouts scoured the desert highways in vain. 'Smittie' was holed up. In due course, it was seen he could not make the sidecar record either so gradually the puzzled scouts returned to the city.

"Next day the transcontinentalist came calmly into town. As he explained his reason for stopping the referee who had waited to check him in started to laugh. Then, and only then, did 'Smittie' get the incorrect figures out of his head. He laughed and he said, 'Well, I have to break it going back.' And almost as simply as that, he did.

"Fearing another lapse of memory due to fatigue he put a very brief schedule on his machine. But the part he considered the most important was a big 89 on the bottom sheet. 'I'll bet I can see that,' he confided to the same referee, Al Koogler, who checked him out.

"At the starting point, by Selig Zoo, 'Smittie's' chief worry was to keep standing up until the very moment of departure. He confided that coming out he had been 'awful tired of sitting down.' 'I thought part of me was dead,' he added with the Smith chuckle.

"The machine which had come through without trouble saw no work or repairs during the layover. His tires were worn but he had faith in them. He started back just as he landed.

"Then about four days later came the terse wire. "Smittie" had made it. No trouble. His Indian Chief was number CCE-585MY and he had a stock Indian sidecar. He used Firestone tires, Splitdorf plugs and magneto, Duckworth chains, and Valvoline oil."

Incidentally, Smittie's record lasted only 12 days before Harley sidecar riders Bill Connelly and Fred Dauria cut about 20 hours off the record.

Did you catch the bit about the scout riders sent out to meet Smittie? These weren't "Scout" riders (unless they just happened to be on Scouts); they were "scout" riders, lowercase *s*, guys who would show Smittie the way. In 1935, roads still weren't marked clearly enough for transcontinental travel. You needed your *Blue Book* of detailed directions or a scout.

There was a lot more pavement on the open roads. The Indian engineering staff had battled continuously to keep the Wigwam products capable of road riding that involved longer and longer stretches of faster and faster going on these new paved roads. The 1935 record of the Whiting brothers and the 1936 record of Smitty showed the tiny engineering staff had done the job.

Chapter 5

Mixed Results
1937–1939

In 1937 Harley-Davidson's new overhead-valve big twin became the official top-speed and long-haul champion. In January 1937 at Daytona Beach, Joe Petrali piloted a highly modified Harley-Davidson Knucklehead to a new American record of 136.183 miles per hour. This ended Indian's bragging rights established with the 1926 record of 132 miles per hour by Johnny Seymour on an eight-valve Indian twin. While they were at it, the Harley crew trucked a 45 side-valve twin to the beach and Petrali rode it to a Class C (stock) record of 102.047 miles per hour.

In April 1937, motorcycle Patrolman Fred Ham rode a Harley-Davidson Knucklehead to a 24-hour record of 1,825 miles (an average of 76

The headline 1938 feature was the tank-top instrument panel. The gray-and-red instruments were unique to 1938. Most of the "buffalo" ignition switches were gray as advertised, but this amber switch and a black switch were also used after stocks of gray switches were exhausted. The one-year-only switch accepts a simple flat-sided key—it's like many luggage keys. Few if any gearshift knobs were gray; archival photos of production models always show a black shift knob.

Amazingly, unrestored Indians continue to surface. This 1938 Chief came with a complete tool kit, rider's instruction book, and sales literature. With paint applied to the rusted cylinders and some touch up to the front fender striping, it was ready to roll.

On the 1938 Chief, the headlight had a low mounting on the new fork shield instead of on the handlebars, and the light was secured to a different bracket. Gray handgrips were standard. The full-color Indian-head transfer on the tanks was first offered on late-1937 models.

miles per hour). The previous American record of 1,562.54 miles (65 miles per hour) belonged to Wells Bennett, who had turned the trick on a Henderson Four in 1922 at the old Tacoma, Washington, board track. Ham, who did all of the riding, bested the international record set by a team of four Frenchmen. Ham also set AMA records for 43 intermediate distances of 50 to 1,800 miles.

Of the two record outings, the Daytona Beach runs were the more glamorous, but the 24-hour record was arguably more meaningful. Clearly, with little or no special preparation the average Harley dealer could go out the next day and better any such Indian factory-sponsored long-distance record. All that was needed was a suitable rider

because the issue of the relative Indian and Harley high-speed long-haul merits had been decided once and for all in Harley-Davidson's favor. After the 1937 Harley-Davidson 24-hour record, Indian made no more long-distance record attempts with the side-valve Chief.

1937 Chief Features

A forward-mounted gearshift lever and rear fenders with larger valances highlighted the styling changes of the 1937 Chief. The new shifter location applied to all models, but the larger valances applied only to the Chief, Standard Scout, and Four. Another styling theme was chrome plating on many small parts. All Chiefs were now fitted with Y motors. The front and rear wheels were interchangeable, and cadmium plating was optional.

Several parts were chrome-plated, including the instrument panel, gearshift lever, forward saddle connector, generator head band, seat post, valve-spring covers, and front and rear exhaust tubes. Although not shown in the *1937 Price List Indian Motocycles*, chrome-plated rims were probably also available as part of the special ordering practice because chrome rims were listed in the 1936, 1939, and 1941 price lists. The chain guard was constructed in two pieces and featured more coverage. The Chief rear fender valance was increased by spot welding sections to the main fender stamping.

A different cast-iron piston was used, but the details are unknown. The oil pump had a different plunger diameter. Late-1937 Chiefs had a new clutch-release worm with a coarser thread. The worm was quicker acting and had been popular in its earlier role as a racing part. The late-1937 worm and nut were not used on 1938 and later models. The reason is that the quicker-acting worm and worm nut were cut at a "steeper" angle, and the new angle did not provide the self-locking feature normally found in a worm-and-worm-nut arrangement. Road riders who had a habit of keeping their motorcycle in gear while stopped in traffic sometimes had their clutch gradually re-engage.

Custom Orders During the 1930s

Custom paint colors and options were the rule, not the exception, on Indian motorcycles in the 1930s. From the Springfield *Sunday Union and Republican*, April 11, 1937: "If you think that some

The T oil lines used on 1936 and 1937 Chiefs were eliminated in 1938. As a concession to practicality the restorer painted the cylinders black, because the dull nickel plating used by Indian was quick to rust. The fuller chain guard came out on the 1937 Chief. For 1938, the stoplight switch was mounted to a new bracket integral with the chain guard.

These cylinder heads were a late-1938 change and differ by having a larger base to match up with the large cylinder fins. The cylinders have two full-sized lower fins on the exhaust stacks instead of two minifins. The oil pump accommodates an integral distributor drive. On early-1938 models the oil pump didn't have the boss (protrusion or, pardon the expression, tit) at the 10 o'clock position.

cars come in flashy colors you should see the myriad color combinations motorcycles are painted—black and red, blue and white, yellow and red, orange and blue, almost every color in the rainbow, except purple. And you could probably have that if you wanted it.

"There is sound reasoning behind this. Let Burton E. (Bud) Acker, the amiable young man who acted as guide through the seven-mile tour of the plant, explain. (There actually are seven miles to

cover in order to see all five floors of the plant, Bud assures you.) 'A motorcycle is a sport article,' Bud points out. 'To be successful in selling it you must cater to the sporting trade and give the buyer exactly what he wants. In a car you take pretty much what you get. But here, we give any combination of parts, colors, motor jobs or accessories asked for. We can do this because we build every machine only on order. The one exception is a new low-priced job in a single color scheme we brought out last year and which has proven extremely popular. Otherwise, every order calls for something different from the next one.'

"He held up a large tag attached to a machine in the process of being assembled. 'With every order a tag like this is made up calling for special combinations of color, accessories, engine job, lights, or anything that the buyer wants. Individual orders for the necessary parts go to the different departments to be made up. Then when the machine is assembled all the parts the order calls for are on hand."

1938: Styling Updates

The headline feature for 1938 was the tank-top instrument panel on the Chief, Four, and Sport Scout. The speedometer, ammeter, and ignition switch were one-year only items. To accommodate the panel, the top frame tube was flattened and a casting was added. For the first time, a speedometer was standard equipment (except on the Junior Scout, for which the speedometer remained an option).

Early publicity photos showed the traditional gold Indian head on the tanks with black Indian script; these were now optional. The standard offering was a pair of full-color Indian heads with black script. Another new tank option was the gold Indian figurehead with the word *Indian* matching the tank paint. This was achieved by having the Indian script clear so that the tank color would show through. An additional midseason option was a pair of silver Indian heads. The saddle front connection was arched upward near the frame connection and was painted black instead of being chrome-plated. The front connection was slotted to mate with the rear saddle connection, permitting fore and aft saddle adjustment. The saddle top was larger.

Functional Changes

The cylinders had larger valve guides. The valve-spring covers were chrome-plated. The new covers also differed from the 1936–1937 covers in that there were no holes for T oil lines (which were discontinued). Since there was no oil-line accommodation, all eight pieces of these "clamshell" covers were identical; previously there were four right and four left covers. New alloy T-slot pistons were fitted. These were provided to accommodate new rings designed to increase oil mileage.

For battery-ignition Chiefs, a new oil-pump assembly included the distributor drive. For manufacturing ease and styling uniformity, the new oil-pump assembly for magneto-ignition Chiefs had the same body, but added to the body was a distributor hole cap. The new "combination" (my term) oil pump was actually two integrated pumps. The oil supply continued to be pumped by a reciprocating plunger driven by the front camshaft. The oil return was pumped by a two-gear pump driven by the rear camshaft, however.

Early-1938 Chiefs had the crankcase breather tube exiting the oil pump; late-1938 Chiefs had the breather tube exiting the forward section of the cam case cover where it remained ever afterwards. Wraparound cam case covers were fitted (see photos). On early-production Chiefs, the oil compartment of the right tank was vented to the left crankcase. Later Chiefs had the oil-tank breather tube routed externally in order to prevent vacuum from building up in the tank.

In honor of Rollie Free's March 1938 Daytona Beach records (see the Daytona Records section later in this chapter), Indian offered special Daytona motors beginning in late 1938. As with the earlier B motors and Savannah motors, the Daytona motors were built off-line using special assembly and balancing techniques. *Contact Points* No. 472, October 4, 1937, commented, "Features of this motor include: hand-polished valve ports, high-compression (5.6:1) aluminum heads, trunk-type pistons fitted with narrow rings, magneto ignition, clearances to accommodate high speeds, and in addition, competition spark plugs." Incidentally, the motor numbers didn't reflect the Daytona status.

Flywheels and connecting rods were revised for the late-1938 Daytona motors. The late-1938 Daytona flywheels were made from a new alloy called Z Metal, an alloy that was a cross between iron and steel. The flywheels added enough of the required strength of steel without incurring the full penalty of the difficult machining associated with steel.

The cadmium-plated wheel rims were part of the chrome-plating package in 1938. The saddlebags are originals, painstakingly resurrected with saddle soap. The Indian head on the tanks is the best of currently available decals; the original design featured more color on the face and feathers. The finish shown was one of the standard, no-extra-cost choices for 1938 and was the only instance of standard striping in other than gold.

Notice how the cam case cover wraps around the pushrod guides and valve covers. The "wraparound" cover was used on 1938 through early-1947 Chiefs.

Also, the flywheel balance factors were changed for the anticipated faster cruising of the 1939 Chiefs. The counterweights were marked with the letter *Z*. On the front (forked) connecting rod a rib was added to both of the lower rings. A different rear connecting rod also debuted on the late-1938 Daytona Chiefs, but the details are unknown. The Daytona parts were listed in the regular parts book, whereas the earlier B and Savannah parts weren't listed.

The stoplight-switch support was provided by a bracket that was integral with the new rear chain guard—the integral bracket was the only difference from the 1937 chain guard. On Chief rear fenders, an electrical terminal block was mounted. The terminal block was 2 1/8 inches long.

Crankcase Breathing: A Problem Never Solved

The late-1938 Chiefs had the crankcase breather located on the right forward section of the cam case (timing) cover. The late-1938 location and components remained unchanged for the rest of the Chief's production life. It was about time. The late-1938 setup was the eighth version tried in 17 production years up to that point. Apparently Indian V-twin crankcase breathing was never fully satisfactory, and the engineering department simply gave up after the mid-1938 change.

The problem was with the disc flutter valve, the central component of the system. Here's a brief explanation of the Chief crankcase breathing system. Incidentally, in all V-twins with a single crankpin, top dead center and bottom dead center of the two pistons aren't simultaneous because of the angle between the cylinders. But the angle has no impact in terms of the principles, so we'll pretend there's no angle.

At bottom dead center, the pistons begin moving upward, causing a vacuum in the crankcase. A disc flutter valve is sucked inward against its seat on the crankcase. This lowers crankcase vacuum as the pistons continue upward. After the pistons reach top dead center, they begin moving downward, increasing crankcase pressure and forcing oil up the valve guides. To keep the crankcase pressure from being excessive, the disc flutter valve is blown off its crankcase seat and against a cam case cover seat. Crankcase pressure is relieved by escaping through the external breather tube. Simple, huh?

Well, not so simple. The breather disc can have a large hole in the middle, or a small hole, or no hole at all. With no hole or a small hole, crankcase pressure varies from a slight vacuum at low rpm to a slight positive pressure at highway cruising speeds.

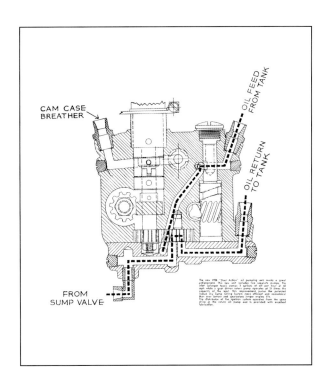

This photo shows the early-1938 oil pump featuring the cam case breather exiting the top rear of the pump. From mid-1938 on, the cam case breather was located on the forward part of the cam case, remote from the pump. Regardless of the location, the breather used a disk flutter valve. The feed pump was a plunger unit, but the return pump was a gear unit

This is the setup if most of the riding is done on the highways, so that the valve guides get positive pressure but not too much pressure, which promotes oil seepage. Conversely, with a large hole, crankcase pressure is slightly positive at low rpm, which is ideal when most riding is done around town, but unsatisfactory at highway speeds where excessive crankcase pressure will produce oil seepage. In other words, the crankcase breathing system worked well over a limited rpm range. Outside the range, you either starved the valve guides with insufficient oil pressure, or you over-pressurized the crankcase and made the engine a weeper.

Daytona Records

In early March, Indian rider Roland "Rollie" Free packed his bags. He had two missions: to beat the Harley-Davidson Class C (stock) 45-cubic-inch (750-cc) motor and to set a new Class C record for motors up to 80 cubic inches (1,300 cc). He knew before he left Indianapolis that he would claim the two records for Indian. The Harley 45-cubic-inch

In March 1938 at Daytona Beach, Rollie Free set a new Class C (stock) record of 109.65 miles per hour on the Chief. The Chief suffered from "wet sumping," so it didn't run the anticipated 115 miles per hour. Too much oil in the crankcase, caused by inadequate oil return, produced a power-robbing "air compressor" effect in the crankcase. Hill/Bentley

record was 102.047 miles per hour, and no 80-cubic-inch Class C record was on the books. Two months before, in secret, Free had been to Daytona Beach and clocked his Sport Scout *Papoose* at 118 miles per hour, while around Indianapolis Free had been street racing his Chief at about 115 miles per hour. Passing through the front door, Free offered a parting remark to his wife, Margaret: "If I don't beat them by 10 miles an hour, I'm not coming back."

The Free speed-tuning technique was "blue-printing," that is, carefully assembling the motor with incremental tightening of the parts, smoothing out the inlet and exhaust ports, and mating the exhaust pipes so smoothly with the ports that there was minimal turbulence. The idea was to approximate as closely as possible the ideals of round pistons, round cylinders, straight bores, 90-degree angles, and parallelism.

Said Free: "I used to tell people you take them apart and get some clean rags. You wipe everything off very carefully and reassemble it carefully—that's all you have to do. Just run it the way they built it. I didn't engineer it; they did. I had a letter from a fel-la in Illinois once, who wanted me to send him some of my rags."

Free ground the valves until they seated with a minimal annular ring of contact, which made the valve heads less angular in cross section. This improved cylinder breathing. But, surprisingly, he didn't change the valve timing.

Some years later, while working on Ed Kretz's racing Sport Scout, here's what happened, according to Free: "Ed Kretz's '38, the best one he had would run about a hundred and seven through Frank Christian's timer. .'. . I said, let's take a regular Bonneville cam. Kretz had a drawer full of those.

In September 1938 at Bonneville, Fred Ludlow upped the Class C (stock) 74-cubic-inch record to 120.747 miles per hour, which gave the big twin a 5-mile-per-hour advantage over the record-setting 45-cubic-inch Sport Scout. This ended the embarrassment of Free's runs, which had shown the Chief to be slower than the Scout.

He said, 'They don't degree out.' I said, 'I don't care whether they degree out or not. What's a couple of degrees?' . . . When I got through with it in three or four evenings, it's a hundred and fourteen. I don't change anything else."

Back to Daytona Beach, March 17, 1938. Free had trouble with the Chief "wet sumping." Wet sumping occurs when the return oil pump is too slow in returning oil from the crankcase to the oil tank. The build-up of excessive oil in the crankcase raises crankcase pressure, which robs power.

On the matter of the Chief running slower than the Sport Scout, Free offered the following: "Well . . . the Chief, the oil wouldn't come out of the bottom. It wouldn't dry sump. The first run at Daytona in '38 to check the bikes was the Chief because everything was on it but the license plate—everything. And it was a hundred and fourteen-something through the Daytona timer. So I thought, well I'll run it while it's warm, you know. Well, that was a mistake; it didn't help it. It had 50 [weight] oil in it and in Indianapolis it worked, out on the road. The

bike would run a hundred fourteen, fifteen. . . . The Chief was a very odd engine because you had such an extreme stroke, three and a quarter by four and seven-sixteenths. . . . The Chief deal, the reason it was slower in my case, was because of the oil in the crankcase, which wouldn't dry sump. Of course, when we got home, I rearranged the deal in the crankcase so it would dry sump readily, and the Chief would run a hundred and fourteen, fifteen, or sixteen miles an hour. That was one I wiped off with clean rags."

The beach conditions weren't ideal. Free continued: "When I got to Daytona, it was hot. The beach was lousy. See, Harley waited for six days, or I don't remember if it was six days or six weeks for a perfect beach down there, for the moon and tide. . . . When I ran it, it [the beach] was so rough that the fuel would come out of the bowl of the Scout in the middle of the mile and cut out and come back on again. I'm talking about a real rough beach."

Even with these problems, Rollie Free ran the Chief 109.65 miles per hour and the Sport Scout

69

111.55 miles per hour, both records. The Sport Scout bettered the Harley Forty-five mark by only 9 1/2 miles per hour, so Rollie didn't measure up to his prebeach boast of 10 miles per hour or else. Strong crosswinds, described by *The Motorcyclist* as "a trifle shifty," gave Free a good excuse for returning to Indianapolis.

1939: World's Fair Styling and Metallic Paints

The New York World's Fair promised a bright tomorrow for a nation eager to be optimistic again. Opened by President Roosevelt on the 150th anniversary of Washington's inauguration, the fair brought the first public displays of nylon, home air conditioning, and television.

Capitalizing on the highly publicized event, Indian introduced the "World's Fair" tank paint scheme as standard. The V tank panel remained optional. Among color choices were Metallic Blue and Silver, Metallic Sand Taupe, and Chinese Red. Except for silver, which had been available for several years, this was the first use of metallics. Small parts throughout the motorcycle were cadmium-plated; previously these had been nickel-plated.

The 1939 leaf-spring fork featured an additional rebound leaf. Some of the spring leaves were narrowed, while the bottom "pickup" leaves were strengthened. A front fork change explains why a number of today's restored leaf-spring Indians are rougher riders than they should be.

Another unrestored gem is this 1939 Chief. The World's Fair paint scheme was unique to the 1939 models, while the V tank panel was still optional. The leaf-spring fork featured an additional rebound leaf. Some of the spring leaves were made narrower, while the bottom "pickup" leaves were strengthened.

Take a deep breath; what follows is a long but necessary explanation.

Leaf-Spring Fork Operation

For 1939 only, Indian added a spring wedge beneath the spring leaves in order to angle the leaves more steeply upward. This was done to increase the upward inclination of the fork rockers, which carried the front axle and the connecting links that joined the rockers to the spring leaves. The purpose was to make the ride softer. "Aha!" you say. "This made the ride softer because the more upwardly inclined rockers gave more fore-and-aft movement to the wheel." This is true, but this is also a minor part of the improved ride.

The geometry of the fork rockers in conjunction with the connecting links is similar to that of an engine connecting rod in conjunction with the crankshaft throw or crankpin (where the rod attaches to the crankshaft). In an engine, piston speed varies throughout the rotation cycle, with maximum speed occurring when the angle between the connecting rod and the crankpin is about 90 degrees. Because of this effect, the piston moves farther in the cylinder's bore for each degree of crankshaft rotation when the angle between the rod and crankpin is near 90 degrees (which occurs around midstroke) than when the angle is near 0 degrees or 180 degrees (which occurs at the top and bottom of the stroke). In the same way, when the angle between the fork rockers and connecting links on a leaf-spring front fork is near 90 degrees, the connecting links deflect the spring leaves more for each incremental movement of the front wheel than when the angle is shallower or steeper. In other words, each inch of wheel travel will deflect the leaf springs the greatest number of inches when the angle between the rockers and connecting links is 90 degrees, and will deflect the springs decreasingly fewer inches as the angle grows greater than 90 degrees. Springs are rated in pounds per inch of deflection, so the greater deflection for each increment of wheel movement at the 90-degree angle takes greater force, resulting in a stiffer effective spring rate at the 90-degree angle than at any other angle. Taking this into account, Indian fitted a spring wedge for 1939 that increased the angle between rockers and connecting links to an angle greater than 90 degrees, resulting in a softer ride for the first part of wheel travel. As the wheel hits bumps, it moves upward, the springs are pulled downward, and the angle between rockers and connecting links shrinks closer and closer to 90 degrees, which increases the effective spring rate. The result is a smooth ride over small bumps and progressively stiffer spring action to prevent the fork from bottoming over large bumps.

What often is the case with improperly restored leaf-spring forks is that they are set up at no load with the rockers and connecting links already forming an angle of about 90 degrees—sometimes even less. The critical angle is further reduced (made worse) as soon as the rider sits in the saddle. This means that the spring action is at its stiffest for the smallest bumps. On the other hand, a large bump is likely to produce almost instantaneous bottoming of the springs as they meet progressively less resistance. This happens because the rockers and connecting links quickly are oriented at less than 90 degrees. Then, on recoil, with too little resistance to slow down the movement, the front end is violently heaved upward. In other words, you pay for this mistake coming and going.

So why did Indian introduce the spring wedge in 1939, and why was it used one year only? The reason for the spring wedge was that Indian had let the weight of the Chief (and Four) grow without taking into consideration the fork geometry issue. In other words, the weight growth sneaked up. With the extra weight, under no load, the front fork rockers had over the years become about 90 degrees apart from the connecting links, instead of the more-than-90-degree relationship that had originally been designed into the fork. Why was the spring wedge used only in 1939? Because a completely new fork for 1940 incorporated the correct geometry without the need for a separate wedge. Incidentally, this was Indian's second lap around the course, the Wigwam having first increased the rocker angle in 1924.

1939, Meanwhile Back at the Ranch

On the front and rear brakes, the linings were of molded material instead of woven material. Less pedal pressure and softer brake action were claimed. Repairs were also made easier because the brake shoes were molded into a curved position. For the front-wheel brake, the cable stop was fitted with a bell-mouth adjusting screw, which allowed more freedom of cable movement at the screw point and prevented cracking.

The standard issue speedometer was black with white numerals and markings and had a maximum indication of 130 miles per hour (instead of 120 miles per hour). The standard speedometer didn't have a maximum-speed hand, but the optional speedometer did. The ammeter was black with white numerals and markings. The black ignition switch featured a tumbler lock with 200 possible key changes. A conventional key replaced the simple flat-strip key of 1938. The key was removable in both the "off" and "park" positions. The switch didn't have the so-called "buffalo head" styling, and set the style for all future Chief ignition switches.

The gasoline-tank caps included a spring-loaded needle valve. In some cases high-speed running was impaired by these spring-loaded caps because the spring pressure was excessive, which resulted in a vacuum in the tanks and interrupted fuel flow. The factory recommended cutting off one to one-and-a-half coils of the spring to reduce the pressure. The oil-tank breather was rerouted to the outside instead of to the left crankcase. This was a late-1938 change announced as a 1939 improvement and was done to prevent a vacuum from building up in the oil tank.

A circular air cleaner replaced the former arrow-shaped air horn; there was no assembly-level factory number for the multipart unit. The Bonneville Chief (the new high-output version of the Chief engine) got its own new Schebler carburetor. The seat-post operation was changed to provide softer action. On the kickstarter, a different pinion featured a clutch with more teeth (number not specified), in order to provide quicker starter-lever engagement and a fuller starter stroke.

The wiring harness was heavier, with 41 strands in each cable instead of 26. The wiring was covered with a more abrasive-resistant coating, and the color codes were made more prominent. Soft rubber tubes covered the wiring exiting the right and left handlebars and headlight shell. Improved wiring clips were fitted. A high-output Auto-Lite generator with a two-step regulator was an option. A revised Willard battery had the plates closer together to prevent plate movement, and reinforcement ribs were built into the battery base to reduce plate movement and post breakage. The battery posts were changed and welded more securely, and a brace was added (to what, Indian didn't say) to prevent movement of the battery in its cradle.

A larger electrical-terminal block was mounted on the rear fender; this block was 2 11/16 inches long instead of 2 1/8 inches long. The larger size was to further separate the terminals and lessen the likelihood of shorting out due to water or dirt. Also on the rear fender was a chrome rear bumper, the same one later used on the skirted-fender models. The taillight lens had a beehive pattern, and the red portion wasn't as dark as before.

On models with the four-speed transmission, the shifter cam and segment were beefed up (this was a running change). The exhaust system had revised styling, including larger exhaust pipes, an upswept chrome-plated tailpipe, and a quieter muffler.

New Bonneville Motors and Changes to Standard Motors

The sportier Chief (and Sport Scout) engines were now labeled "Bonneville" motors in honor of Fred Ludlow's September 1938 record runs on the Utah salt flats. Ludlow scooted 120.747 miles per hour on the Chief, a Class C stock record for up to 80-cubic-inch (1,300-cc) motorcycles. Incidentally, Ludlow also upped the Sport Scout ante to 115.125 miles per hour. This ended the embarrassment of the March 1938 Daytona Beach record runs in which Rollie Free had gone faster on the Sport Scout than on the Chief. Bonneville motors featured a number of new parts, and each Bonneville motor was block tested to ensure adequate power output before installation in a frame.

To illustrate the pecking order among Chiefs, here are the 1938 retail prices: Chief, battery ignition, $385; Chief, magneto ignition, $400; Chief, magneto ignition with Daytona motor, $425. So, the Daytona Chief cost about 10 percent more than the cheapest Chief. As with the earlier B and Savannah fast motors, there was no special motor numbering system for the Daytona engines.

Front and rear cylinder heads, standard and Bonneville, featured a larger base that blended in with the cylinder fins. Bonneville heads yielded higher compression, 6.2:1 instead of 5.6:1 (1938 Daytona Motors). Almost all 1939 Chief heads were no longer of the Ricardo style. A few Ricardo heads with the 1939-style large base have turned up at swap meets, so either a few late-1938 or early-1939 Chiefs had these crossbreeds, or the crossbreeds were for the commercial Traffic Car. The non-Ricardo heads improved engine breathing, claimed the factory. The compression ratio remained 5.3:1 on the standard heads.

All Chief motors were equipped with new medium-range Indian C-14 spark plugs. Although identical in appearance to the 1938 Standard and Daytona cylinder assemblies, the 1939 jugs had new valve guides. Bonneville heads had polished inlet and exhaust ports. Two-piece screw-on cadmium-plated valve covers replaced the four-piece clipped-on chrome-plated covers used in 1938. The cylinders had a "mirror finish" bore and improved porting, and together with the new heads, revised cam profiles, and different valve lifters, accounted for a 3 to 5-mile-per-hour increase in top speed.

The cylinder heads with enlarged bases were phased in on late-1938 Chiefs but were cataloged as 1939 parts. This finish, Metallic Sand Taupe and Chinese Red, was one of the standard no-extra-cost choices for 1939. Prior to 1939, the only metallic offering was silver.

Indian offered this three-wheeled Chief, termed the Traffic Car, for heavy-duty commercial work, as seen in this example restored by Essex Motorsports. Some had bodies that extended forward over the steering head, providing weather protection for the rider.

Whoopee. That was the party line, but the factory didn't say whether that speed margin applied to the standard motor, the Bonneville motor, or both.

New standard and Bonneville cams had revised profiles in order to lower the acceleration during lift and reduce deceleration during closing. These changes increased valvetrain life, provided quieter operation, and contributed to the increased top speed. Indian claimed the 1939 standard motors were as fast as the 1938 Daytona motors. Different valve-spring collars were fitted on the standard motors to work with a different split-key.

On Bonneville motors, double valve springs provided better cam following at higher engine speeds. Each double-spring set consisted of the regular valve spring mounted in the outer position and a new inner spring. Keeping the springs in place were new Bonneville collars, also with a split-key for each collar. On both standard and Bonneville motors, the valve stems were revised to work with the new collars. Standard and Bonneville Chiefs used a new inlet valve.

Standard and Bonneville alloy pistons had a different cam profile, that is, a different eccentricity that under heat distortion would become more circular than with the previous cam profile. Each piston used three plain compression rings instead of two notched rings, but the single oil-control ring on each piston was unchanged. The new compression rings had less wall tension and were Ferrox treated to prevent scuffing during the break-in period.

New Bonneville connecting rods were announced, along with the admission that these had been used on late-1938 Daytona motors. The front (forked) rod had a reinforcing rib added to each ring. The aluminum roller retainers used from 1935 through 1938 were replaced by the steel retainers that had been used from 1927 through 1934.

Another late-1938 Daytona feature applied to both standard and Bonneville motors for 1939. The flywheels were made of Z Metal. The balance factors for the flywheels were changed for the anticipated faster cruising speeds of the 1939 Chiefs, and the counterweights were marked with the letter Z.

The right crankcase assembly had new pushrod guides, which were threaded in order to accept screw-on valve covers. The left crankcase assembly was different, although the factory number wasn't changed. The left case didn't accept the oil-tank breather tube through the breather-tube elbow. There was no breather-tube elbow or elbow plug listed. In other words, the former hole was left undrilled and untapped.

A running change brought new standard and Bonneville inlet-valve pushrods on late-1939 motors. These had a groove 1/32 inch deep and 1/16 inch wide ground lengthwise to increase oiling of the inlet valve and guide.

The oil pump had a different body, feed-tube elbow, and feed-tube assembly. The oil-pump body had a more square shape and had a boss on the upper left (purpose unknown). The oiling system had a revised sump-valve back plate, the hole on

which was reduced in diameter and moved as low as possible. This was to ensure that the oil stayed below the level of the flywheels. The optional four-speed transmission had a stronger shifter cam. Likewise, the new shifter segment was stronger. The frame was renumbered because the seat post had a new bushing.

Mixed Results

The 1937, 1938, and 1939 seasons brought mixed results. On the plus side, Indian racing glory—almost totally won with the 45-cubic-inch Sport Scout—helped by shining a halo over the rest of the line-up. At the national championship level, Sport Scouts had generally outperformed the Harley-Davidson Forty-five. The Chief did its bit by twice setting Class C (stock) records. The homely upside-down Four was replaced by the beautiful 1938 Four, and although the Four remained a small seller, it shined some halo glow over the Chief. The open-fender styling was brought to its zenith on the 1938 and 1939 Indians.

On the minus side were several factors. Harley's Sixty-one overhead-valve (Knucklehead) further strengthened Milwaukee's dominance of the all-important big-twin field. Milwaukee's overhead-valve big twins opened up an entirely new evolutionary path with a bright future, but Indian's side-valve twins had come to a technical dead end. The Harley-Davidson overhead-valve EL had become America's fastest motorcycle and had the Class A (unrestricted) record to prove it. Indian no longer had the only claim to dry-sump lubrication, and the Chief's sliding-gear transmission compared poorly to Harley's new constant-mesh gearbox. In the styling arena, Springfield had been two years late with the tank-top instrument panel spawned by the 1936 Model EL, today known as the Knucklehead. Not many riders changed brands, as brand loyalty ran deep; but Indian was facing a tougher time of recruiting from among the great unwashed. Indian needed something dramatic, perhaps revolutionary.

Chapter 6

Looks to Kill For
1940–1941

Revolutionary skirted fenders and spring-frame rear suspension were featured in the 1940 Indian line-up. These epic changes redefined the Indian Chief, which ever afterward was pitched as a luxury tourer rather than an all-arounder that could challenge any Harley-Davidson for top speed.

The skirted fenders are popular with today's collectors and motorcyclists in general, but these skirts were love-hate things in their day. In late 1939, Frank Christian worked in Floyd Clymer's Los Angeles Indian shop as a mechanic. With the impending takeover of the dealership by Johnson Motors, Christian recalled, "I just could not

The black ammeter shown was used, with minor changes, on Chiefs from 1939 through 1946. The 130-mile-per-hour speedometer shown was used on 1939 and 1940 models. This ignition switch shown was introduced on the 1939 models and continued (with minor changes) through the end of the Chief line in 1953. The switch accepts a conventional key, similar to a typical car key. The embossed oil tank cap officially debuted in 1941.

This front-fender light was used on 1940–1946 models. The headlight was mounted to the fork shield with a new-style head-lamp bracket (pedestal). The black oil pump was not standard. The black exhaust system was a replacement unit sold by Indian during World War II.

wait to get out of Clymer's, to get up to that other place with all these new Indians with them skirted fenders—beautiful things!"

Desert enduro rider and speed-run artist Max Bubeck had a different view: "That's when Indian stopped making motorcycles and started making Harleys." Bubeck's objection was the extra weight. For example, the skirted fender Chief was listed at

558 pounds (dry), while the open-fendered 1939 Chief was listed at 481 pounds.

All models got the skirts, while the spring frame was limited to the Chief and the Four. The skirts were bounded by aluminum strips, and short decorative aluminum strips also graced the top of each fender. Although the trim strips would be around for many years, the 1940 strips were unique in having a semicircular cross section. As of this writing, all reproduced fender trim is manufactured in the 1941-and-later pattern with flat sides.

New metal tank emblems replaced the transfers that had been used on previous Chiefs. The new emblems were teardrop-shaped and chrome-plated with "Indian" embossed down the side. They were used on Chiefs for 1940 and 1941 only.

For both styling and engineering reasons, the cylinder heads and cylinders had larger cooling fins with dramatic streamlined styling. For the first time, all forks and frames were black rather than color-matched to the tanks and fenders.

External Changes

The front fork had revised mounting tabs for the skirted fenders and incorporated the required geometry to achieve soft springing without the need of the spring wedge used on 1939 models only. The front fork was longer, 31 inches instead of 29 inches, hence the fork had an increased rake; and the listed wheelbase grew, from 61 1/2 to 62 inches.

Between the two front down tubes was a Purolater oil filter. This was the first use of an oil filter on Indians, but the filter wouldn't be around long. The filter could easily be installed backwards, which slowed oil flow, sometimes blew up the filter, and caused an accumulation of debris around the sump screen and in the oil pump. Even when installed properly, when hot motors cooled off in freezing weather, the resulting condensation would freeze in the filter, clogging it completely. Consequently, the filter was eliminated during the 1940 season by a running change.

Seating was revised for 1940, resulting in a taller saddle height. The saddle top had thicker padding, and seat-post suspension was mandatory. The saddle connection was one-piece, replacing the previous front and rear saddle connections. Solo saddle height increased from 29 to 30 1/2 inches, and buddy-seat height increased from 31 1/2 to 33 inches.

The frame was also revised for 1940. The seat mast (a frame tube that supports the seat post) was nearly vertical instead of having a pronounced rearward inclination. For the accessory buddy seat, the bracket where the buddy-seat springs attached was

The 1940 Chiefs were keynoted by skirted fenders and a spring frame. For the first time, all forks and frames were black. The correct muffler was offset from the tailpipe; some reproduction mufflers are concentric with the pipe. The three-piece exhaust system had a connector section just in front of the rear tube, which joins the front and rear header pipes. The front fender was unique to 1940 because the width from skirt to skirt was the same as the width of the top of the fender. Note the teardrop-shaped metal emblems on the gas tanks. These replaced the transfers that had been used on previous Chiefs. © Hans Halberstadt

A black-painted kickstarter was standard for 1940. The standard tires for 1940 were the 4.50x18-inch size, which had been optional for 1935–1939. Also for 1940, the generator was moved from the front to the back of the seat mast, and the rubber distributor cover was standard (and an accessory thereafter). Footboards were bonded to the base instead of riveted to it.

This 1940 Chief exudes charm because of the understated restoration. Nice touches are the black wheels, black safety guards, and black footboard extenders. Saddlebags and saddle trim are nonstandard, but such rider choices were also made in the motorcycle's era. A 1941 toolbox was fitted. The twist-on Raceway air cleaner became available as an accessory in the late 1940s.

curved to clear a circular fuse block mounted above the generator.

A "Fill-Rite" battery was fitted. This featured a rubber button on the top of each cell that when pushed by the rider forced excess water out of an overfilled cell. These batteries are not currently available to restorers. A wraparound air cleaner was fitted, although early publicity photos didn't show this cleaner. As in 1939, there was no number for an overall cleaner assembly.

As noted earlier, cylinder heads and cylinders sported larger cooling fins and more attractive styling. The 1940 cylinders were the first of the so-called "square base" design, in which the sides of

the base were beefed up, which, in turn, gave the base a more squarish appearance. Standard, low-compression (commercial) and Bonneville cylinders and cylinder heads had different factory numbers because of varying compression ratios. Bonneville cylinders and heads also benefited from polished ports and surfaces. The standard and Bonneville Chiefs were fitted with new Schebler carburetors, the Bonneville featuring a larger float and float bowl.

An optional Edison-Splitdorf magneto was of the rotating magnet (RM) design with a different external appearance (nearly square in outline) than previous magnetos, which had a top that was rounded in outline. (The RM magneto had debuted a year before on Four as an option to battery ignition.)

On the lower right side was a different rear brake control setup. The brake pedal had a curved upper surface, and the pedal stopped on a frame lug instead of the front footboard lug. The pedal was connected to the rear brake by two cadmium-plated rods, joined by a black bell crank slightly to the rear of the kickstarter. The two-piece construction was necessary in order to work with the rear suspension.

The footboards were longer, newly styled with fore-and-aft ribs and no "Indian" label, and were bonded to the base. Bonding eliminated the problem of riveted footboard mats separating from the base. Also, the footboards were nearly horizontal (only slightly inclined) instead of having a pronounced upward tilt. According to the factory, this was possible because the rear suspension made it unnecessary for the rider to "post" (that is, get out of the saddle and stand on the footboards for rough going). The Chief rear footboard mounting tabs were above the frame instead of below the frame.

Another first-time feature was a center stand. When riding, the center stand was maintained in the up position by a latch. The rear stand was

Jade Green, shown here, was a standard color for 1940, along with Kashan Green (blue-green), Seafoam Blue (medium blue), Indian Red, Fallon Brown (tan), and black. Sales catalogs mentioned only red, blue, and black. Typically, the owner has opted for the more-practical black-painted finish on the cylinders instead of the correct nickel-plated finish

By 1940, the Chief was again the most popular Indian for police work. Prior to World War II, 60 percent of the nation's police departments that used motorcycles bought Indians. The winter windshield includes the large black apron. This was the last year for the Indian-face horn. Note that the oversized police generator extends horizontally over the chain guard.

eliminated. Also a first was a "jiffy" stand (side stand, or kickstand) as standard equipment. The jiffy-stand leg was mounted directly to an integral frame casting instead of being clamped to the frame. Since the side stand mounting on all models was built in, midyear instructions were issued by the factory for riders who felt there was insufficient lean provided by the stands. Grinding the stand leg was the answer.

A full chain guard completely encircled the kickstarter pedal. On the Chief, the speedometer drive exited through a rubber tube on the lower forward section of the left side of the rear fender skirt. On each side, the fender was braced to the frame by a black brace having two pronounced bends. In later years these braces gradually assumed a less angular shape. The chrome-plated rear bumper of 1939 was continued. On the rear brake plate, the brake arm was straight when viewed in profile and was black instead of cadmium-plated. Also, the brake arm had a D-shaped hole to mate with the brake mechanism. During the course of 1940-model production, the right and left spring-frame slipper brackets—the parts that held the axle—were modified. A reinforcing rib was welded to the top of each bracket, and different factory numbers were assigned for the stronger brackets. An accessory item was a new black cast-iron luggage rack.

Internal Changes

The front and rear connecting rods introduced on the 1939 Bonneville Chief became standard issue on all 1940 Chiefs. The front (forked) rod had a rib added to each ring; details of the rear (straight) rod are unknown. The Bonneville Chief got a different piston, which was domed. To allow for the higher piston, the Bonneville combustion chamber was relieved 1/8 inch. Bonneville pistons had three new rings that were 3 1/4 inches in diameter, as usual, but were only 1/16 inch in (horizontal) thickness. The latter dimension (two-thirds of the previous 3/32 inch) reduced drag against the cylinder walls. As before, the Bonneville piston had a T-slot to compensate for thermal expansion. The standard Chief continued to use the same three rings as before. Both the standard and Bonneville Chief continued with one oil-control ring per piston. The inlet valve (standard and Bonneville) and exhaust valve (standard or Bonneville) differed from the previous valves by accommodating a revised collar key of unknown details.

The spring frame was 1/4 inch wider at the rear, forcing the rear chain 1/4 inch outward. This was achieved by making both the sprocket driver gear (triple gear) and the transmission main shaft 1/4 inch longer.

Most of the first several hundred Chiefs (and Fours) had rear spring units that didn't work properly. Here's the inside story from former test engineer Allen Carter: "One motorcycle would work, and one wouldn't. If you assembled maybe 12 motorcycles you might have got one that might have been lucky enough to be all right." Carter rigged a pencil, paper, and bracket arrangement and proved the rear suspension barely moved on even severe bumps.

Carter continued: "They were nothing but two things which went in there and which you adjusted

Rare Chief Racing Wins

The 74-cubic-inch (1,200-cc) Chief wasn't Indian's main racing weapon, as most Class C (stock) motorcycle racing was done in the 45-cubic-inch (750-cc) class, in either flat-track or road-racing events. There was another form of Class C racing that permitted side-valve motorcycles up to 80 cubic inches (1,300 cc) and overhead-valve motorcycles up to 61 cubic inches (1,000 cc). These were the so-called TT events, originally termed miniature TT races after the famous Isle of Man Tourist Trophy races in Britain. Riders could enter the 45-cubic-inch TT races or the 80-cubic-inch TT races, and if they wished, riders could use a 45-cubic-inch motorcycle in the 80-cubic-inch races.

The TT races featured at least one right turn and one left turn, plus at least one jump. The short TT courses, typically 1/2 mile long, mimicked road-racing conditions but offered the advantage of full course viewing by the spectators. The TT race courses were also easier to lay out than the deceptively simple-looking flat tracks. Flat tracks, on the other hand, required just the right amount of banking and just the right amount of watering and grading; otherwise either muddy or dusty conditions prevailed. Mud killed sliding ability for the brakeless (yes, brakeless) racers, and dust brought too much danger to the scene. The rules for TT racing permitted brakes, so full-lock slides on perfect dirt weren't essential. Up into the 1950s, many if not most motorcycle races were promoted by local motorcycle clubs, and the relative ease of laying out the TT courses was an attractive feature to these amateur organizations.

Prior to the mid-1936 introduction of Harley-Davidson's 61-cubic-inch overhead-valve big twin (now termed the Knucklehead), most 80-cubic-inch TTs featured the big side-valve Indians and Harleys slugging it out. After the Knuckleheads arrived, most 80-cubic-inch TT races pitted 74-cubic-inch or 80-cubic-inch Chiefs against 61-cubic-inch Knuckleheads.

When ridden by great riders, the Chief was capable of winning important TT races. Ed Kretz Sr. won the 1938 Pacific Coast 80-cubic-inch TT Championship on a Chief. Incidentally, Class C was evolving, and it was not until late 1938 that a TT race was termed a "national championship." In the 1940 season, Ted Edwards won two national championship 80-cubic-inch TT races on a Chief, and Indian advertisements credited the new spring frame as a major asset to racers. Chiefs faded from the top-drawer TT races after that. A rare exception was Bill Meador's win of the 1947 Southwestern TT Championship in his hometown of Waco, Texas. Meador rode a rigid-frame Chief. Jack Colley of Seattle, Washington, also won many northwestern TT races on his postwar spring-frame Chief; but in the postwar era, unlike in the 1930s, regionally titled TT events were a notch down from the national championships.

Chiefs fell from TT favor because of their large size and weight. Apparently, when comparing the Chief and the Sport Scout, the extra weight of the Chief wasn't sufficiently offset by its extra power. The Knucklehead Harleys had more beans to muscle around the extra weight. But by the 1950s, even Harley riders entering the 80-cubic-inch TTs opted for 45-cubic-inch, or starting in 1954, the 55-cubic-inch KH models instead of the big twins. The short and twisty TT races were just too cramped for the big twins, and eventually the TTs were dominated by middle-sized British 40-cubic-inch (650-cc) vertical twins.

---

the chain with, on the back wheel. But all these pieces, the pieces that went on each slider, if you added them all up you would wind up with something [a variance] maybe a sixteenth [of an inch] or better, so this thing when you put in the axle and tightened it up, this would lock up the whole thing."

The problem was the stack up of tolerances on each part in the assembly. Consequently, the right and left slipper brackets and associated hardware were of sufficiently different thicknesses to cause binding once the axle was inserted and tightened down.

"So we finally got that straightened out and then production hollered like heck because the tolerances were too close," Carter added.

Early-production transmission cases included an oil filler plug because the transmission and primary drives had separate oil supplies, a new feature. Effective with Chief motor number CDO-2154M, a hole was drilled to connect the primary drive and transmission, and a single oil supply again serviced both the primary drive and the gearbox. As soon as practical, the oil filler plug was phased out. In other words, some Chiefs may have had the plug even

Samples of state police organizations using Chiefs (numbers of Chiefs in parentheses) included Pennsylvania (602), Massachusetts (237), North Carolina (103), Texas (80), and Maryland (45). Cities using Chiefs include New York (480), Philadelphia (126, including some Scouts), and Boston (100).

when using a common oil supply for the primary drive and transmission. The later transmission cases reverted to the previous factory number.

A 90-Degree Chief Motor

President du Pont took an interest in 90-degree V-twins, so in early 1940, the factory built a 90-degree engine using standard Chief components combined with new right and left crankcase assemblies and other detail changes, as necessary. The 90-degree Chief motor was delivered to Allen Carter in Wilmington, Delaware. Carter had been a du Pont employee in Wilmington since the mid-1920s when the family made Du Pont automobiles.

Carter installed the 90-degree Chief motor in du Pont's personal Morgan three-wheeled car in Wilmington. Meanwhile, Indian and Harley-Davidson were building big twin-powered tricycle ammunition carriers for an army development

program. Indian built two Chief-powered trikes, one a little wider than the other, and both used Model T Ford rear axles cut out for chain drive access. Both companies' trikes were delivered in June. Harley won a follow-up contract for 16 trikes, but Indian's trike program ended.

Du Pont directed Allen Carter to install the 90-degree Chief motor in the wider of the two leftover trikes. Carter did this by cannibalizing parts from the Morgan, including the flywheel, electric starter assembly, transmission, and clutch. Indian's Army liaison staffer, Frank Long, brought in an army colonel and another officer to view the 90-degree trike, and both officers rode it for a considerable time. They were impressed that the trike ran with almost no vibration. The visit had its intended result, a development contract for a vibrationless shaft-drive motorcycle, which would become the 45-cubic-inch Model 841 built in 1941 and tested in 1942. Incidentally, the narrower of the two Indian-powered trikes—the one Allen Carter didn't modify—showed up at a Florida antique motorcycle meet in 1994!

1940 Production

One of the highlights of E. Paul du Pont's presidency was the business year of 1940, which ran from October 1, 1939, through September 30, 1940. After more than a decade of building only one-third of the nation's motorcycles, Indian pulled neck and neck with Harley-Davidson. Indian built 10,431 motorcycles to Harley's 10,855. This was as close as Springfield had come to outproducing Milwaukee since 1921. To meet the production demands, the Wigwam tripled its work force. This production surge, however, was a mirage. Indian's total included 5,000 Chiefs for the French army, a windfall contract the Wigwam received without bidding competition from Harley-Davidson. Domestic production still favored Milwaukee by two to one. Considering the French order and the customary Chief share of civilian production, 1940 saw more Chiefs produced than at any time since the late-1920s.

1941: A Year of Refinements

Decorative aluminum strips were added to the tanks—a short strip in front of the metal nameplate and a long strip behind the nameplate. These strips weren't shown in the sales catalog or the press-release photos because prototype models were used for the photo sessions. Some 1941 models may have been built without the strips.

Optional 5.00x16-inch tires were listed. Indian had argued against these tires in *Indian News*,

Relatively few Indian and Harley-Davidson big twins were built for military use. An exception was an order for 5,000 Chiefs with sidecars for the French army, shipped in early 1940. Most military Indians used in World War II were the 30.50-cubic-inch (500-cc) Model 741, which was similar to the civilian Sport Scout. Bruce Palmer

claiming they introduced handling uncertainties. The factory also knew the rear suspension worked better with the higher-pressure 4.50x18-inch tires than with the lower-pressure 16-inch tires. Many riders had voiced a preference for 5.00x16-inch tires, however, so Indian had to give in. Harley-Davidson staffers must have had a few private laughs, for Harleys with low-pressure 5.00x16-inch

tires had closed most of the comfort gap between the rigid-frame Milwaukee models and the spring-frame Springfield models.

In the tank-top instrument panel, a 110-mile-per-hour speedometer replaced the previous 130-mile-per-hour unit. The black face and white lettering were continued, and the speedometer was standard issue without a maximum-speed hand. A

Indian and Harley-Davidson built a few big twin–powered prototype tricycles for an Army testing program at Camp Holabird, Maryland. Testing began in summer 1940. The Army didn't like the trikes' handling. The four-wheeled Jeep killed trike prospects. Jimmy Hill

Very rare today, this Chief is in unrestored original trim. On the 1941 Chief, the front fender width was 6 3/8 inches from skirt to skirt, a 1/8-inch increase achieved by rolling the skirt edges where they join the fender center. The extra width accommodated the 5.00x16-inch tires that became optional in 1941. Likewise, the front forks were 1/8 inch wider. Flat-sided fender trim replaced trim of semicircular cross section. The horn face and handgrips were new for 1941. ©Hans Halberstadt

The 1941 models were fitted with aluminum strips on the tanks (but some early-production units may not have had the strips). Also new for the year: the front fork shield extends to the bottom of the spring leaves, and the headlight bucket was chrome-plated and housed a sealed-beam lamp. The headlight wiring passes through a different pedestal instead of the light body. ©Hans Halberstadt

new ammeter (still with the same factory number) had the legend "HOYT METER." To make the ride even more comfortable, additional saddle padding was provided. For the first time, the carburetor was listed as a Linkert model, and the carburetor was painted in aluminum lacquer instead of black. A black front safety (crash) guard was mandatory, at least in some areas, as revealed in a factory-to-dealer *1941 Price List*. The sales catalog and press-release photos didn't show the front guard. This was because of the use of prototypes for the advance publicity photos, or because the standard equipment groups may have differed according to

Bob Hallowell was congratulated after winning the 1941 National Championship TT in Chattanooga, Tennessee. Most TT courses were about 1/2 mile per lap. The 74-cubic-inch Chiefs and 61-cubic-inch and 74-cubic-inch Harley big twins gradually fell out of favor for TT racing after World War II when riders of 45-cubic-inch models began to turn faster laps on the tight courses. Indian News, published from 1926 through 1947 (except in 1933), was given to all registered Indian owners.

Shown on this 1942 Chief is one of the two-color finishes that were optional at extra cost. This 1942 example is in Fallon Brown and red. In 1941, several two-color finishes were offered at no extra cost.

geographical area and local preferences. A chrome-plated guard was available as an accessory item.

There were several functional changes. New valve guides were made of a harder alloy, permitting tighter clearances and reduced wear. Since the guides were stocked and shipped as part of the cylinder assembly, the cylinder assemblies were renumbered, with different factory numbers for standard, Bonneville, and low-compression (commercial) Chiefs. The 1941 pistons were 4 ounces lighter, which called for new balancing instructions. The pistons had the T slot lower in the skirt. The oil-pump assemblies (battery and magneto ignition) were renumbered because of a larger feed-pump plunger that increased flow by 57 percent. The larger plunger diameter also required a new number for the oil-pump body common to both types. The C-14 spark plugs were said to conduct heat better. The wiring system was changed to isolate the generator circuit from the circuits for the main lights and stoplight, using a fuse in each of the latter circuits.

A War Economy

As early as January 1941, a year before the United States entered World War II, steel producers were indefinitely delaying shipments of metal for nondefense orders. Producers were maximizing profits by selling to the federal government. At the same time, the government had complete control over distribution. So, practically speaking, nondefense orders were canceled. Even military motorcycle construction was held up because the government had higher delivery priorities for planes, ships, and tanks. Indian received about half the orders for military motorcycles that Harley-Davidson received and so finished the business year (September 1941) with a total of 8,739 motorcycles built, versus Harley's 18,428.

Skirted-fender styling was Indian's bid at keeping competitive with Harley-Davidson in 1940 and 1941. After all, skirted-fender styling was cheaper than a total engineering rework of the Chief, which needed an overhead-valve engine

In the year or so prior to the United States' entry into World War II, civil defense units were popular. These men and the young mascot are members of the Albany, New York, Patroon mounted guard. Second from right is Brownie Betar, noted hill-climber. Second from left is Tom Paradise, builder of top hill-climb Indians. Butch Baer collection

and a constant-mesh transmission to compete on a strictly technical level. Given Indian's financial weakness, the revolutionary styling turned out to be masterful business strategy as well as masterful art.

Ed Kretz looks worried in this prewar California TT because he had lost the oil cap and oil was all over him and his Chief. A spectator tries to hand Kretz a replacement. In early 1942 the AMA canceled racing for the duration of the war. Ed Kretz collection

Chapter 7

Drafted
1942–1945

A war economy had already been functioning for about a year before the United States entered World War II on December 7, 1941. Two months after America joined the fighting, the government officially took over control of all heavy industries and much of everyday life. All civilian automobile production was halted in February. In May, a national 35-mile-per-hour speed limit was established and the fuel supplies of 17 eastern states were cut in half. In December, nationwide gasoline rationing was established. The main purpose of gas rationing was to eliminate tire wear because the Japanese had taken over the rubber plantations of East Asia. In 1943, the Office of Price Administration banned all nonessential driving in 17 eastern states. In 1944, gasoline rationing was reduced to 2 gallons a week.

The military draft priority was for young men. Chances of being drafted were reduced for those over 30, so most dealers weren't drafted. Some dealers with large shop facilities were able to take on military subcontracts, which further reduced their likelihood of being drafted. Some young men had their drafts deferred because they held jobs deemed essential to national defense. These included railroaders, steel workers, and aircraft plant workers.

There were no organized motorcycling activities such as racing or group touring during the war years. Gas rationing

During the war, all new motorcycle sales required government approval. As a result, most were sold to police departments. Some wartime Chiefs carried on with nickel-plated cylinders from leftover stock, but later wartime Chiefs had black cylinders like this example. Chrome was minimized or eliminated. Many smaller parts were Parkerized—chemically treated to a dull finish—which was even cheaper than painting them.

The horn face on the wartime Chiefs was the same as used on the 1941 and 1942 Chiefs, but was black instead of chrome-plated. Likewise, black finish was applied to the instrument panel and the tank caps. On some motorcycles, the following parts were Parkerized: wheel hubs, front-fork spring leaves, front and rear brake plates, clutch pedal, brake pedal, and rear brake lever.

made motorcycle riding a limited and cherished privilege. A few crafty guys learned that they could make a motorcycle run on such juices as kerosene and parts-cleaning solvent. The bikes ran poorly, but, hey, they ran, and you weren't limited to two gallons a week.

The AMA's official magazine, *The Motorcyclist*, carried on, although its page count eventually fell to only 16 pages, half of the prewar size. Content included maintenance tips to keep those irreplaceable bikes going, reminiscences of happy prewar days, and, always, letters from the boys overseas

who yearned to get back in the saddle. The editors were undoubtedly challenged to fill up the pages. In a preview of the postwar motorcycle climate, the magazine printed a number of letters from American fighting men suggesting that British and European motorcycles were the wave of the future. Indian and Harley-Davidson ran ads in *The Motorcyclist* and in such magazines as *Mechanics Illustrated* and *Popular Mechanics*. The ads had three themes: the rugged performance of Indians and Harleys in military use, the motorcycle companies' patriotic war contributions, and the exciting prospects for advanced models once victory was achieved.

1942: Token Production, Cosmetic Changes

Few 1942 models were built because of government restrictions during 1941 that affected aluminum and steel. Then, on February 9, 1942, the government halted all civilian production. No 1942 sales literature was printed; however, several issues of *Indian News* and *Indian Dealer Bulletin* Number 504 of October 3, 1941, shed light on the 1942 models.

Indian Dealer Bulletin Number 504 announced the end of Four and Thirty-Fifty production. The exact timing of the production halt on the Four is unclear because some Fours have survived with 1942 motor numbers having the DDB prefix.

Indian-head tank emblems were used on the Chief, which can be verified by *Indian News* photographs. These tank emblems were used on Chiefs through 1946. According to *Indian Dealer Bulletin* Number 504, some 1941 motor and frame numbers were used on 1942 models built after October 3, when normally all models in production would be for the next season. Chiefs, Fours, and Sport Scouts, however, have survived with the 1942 motor number prefixes of CDB, DDB, and FDB, respectively. That same bulletin stated that there were no major changes planned for the reduced line-up of the Chief and Sport Scout.

Indian's Wartime Production Problems

Former test engineer Allen Carter related how the war brought special problems to the Wigwam: "One of the worst things was, we didn't have a good enough standing that we could use virgin material. . . . [P]eople would turn in pots and pans, and we used all this secondary aluminum, like pistons. God almighty! We had a terrible time getting through that thing.

"Our cylinder heads on a Seventy-four for the Army—we were building those to go to Russia— Seventy-fours with a sidecar, and part of the specifications was, it had to maintain 55 miles an hour with a 500-pound weight in the sidecar. Boy, that was a job! We couldn't do that, because what would happen, these cylinder heads were made out of secondary aluminum, and we would blow holes and the spark plugs would come right out of that thing. They would get so damned hot that they would burn a hole right at the spark plug, and it blew the plug out and you would have a hole in the cylinder head [as big as a 50-cent piece]. The pistons, we had to allow, oh, about a thousandth more on the piston clearance than you would on a regular piston. So we had ring problems; we had oil problems . . . we had a lot of problems."

During the testing for the Russian project, oiling problems were also discovered. To maintain the required 55 miles per hour with sidecar gearing meant long periods of running at more than 3,000 rpm. Carter learned that the traditional plunger oil pump lost all flow under this circumstance. He then tested for cold-weather operation, using dry ice packed around the pump and oil lines, and likewise determined the plunger pump was ineffective. Indian squeaked by with the Russian contract, but as a result of the oil-pump tests, plans were begun for a gear-driven pump that would be a postwar replacement. In fact, a cast-iron gear-driven pump was completed and tested during the war and found entirely satisfactory under the same conditions that had thwarted the plunger pump.

Even the simplest problem could hold up military production. The U.S. Army contracts called for a complete tool kit to be supplied with each motorcycle. All well and good, except that Indian was out of its special valve-cover pliers built with serrated gripping surfaces that mated with the valve-cover diameters. These special pliers had been designed and built back in the 1920s when Indian was much bigger and more prosperous. But by the 1940s, Indian was so financially strapped it could afford neither a large nor a small cost-efficient order for the pliers. Without the valve-cover pliers, Indians were going into storage instead of being delivered. Allen Carter went to a local store and bought a pair of water-pump (plumber's) pliers. He then contacted the manufacturer, who was only too willing to cut 2 1/2 inches off the pliers' handles so the tool would fit in the toolbox because the war had stopped sales of this item in the civilian market. Barrels of short pliers were soon received, and the motorcycle-delivery crisis was over.

1943–1945: The Chief Becomes the Only Model

By 1944, the Chief became the only model in production. Civilian sales were limited to police departments and other "essential" purposes such as commuting to defense jobs and commercial uses connected with the defense industry. In practice, almost all civilian sales were for police use.

The Harley-Davidson archives reveal that during 1943 the government permitted 137 police departments to purchase new Harleys. Since police business was, roughly, a 50-50 split between Milwaukee and Springfield, a similar number of departments probably were allowed to buy new Indians.

Here's how the red tape worked: The police department placed its order with the local Indian dealer. Additionally, the police chief, the mayor, or the purchasing agent wrote a letter to the dealer explaining why the new motorcycles were needed. The letter had to include a listing of the mileage of used police motorcycles that were to be traded in. The dealer then forwarded to the factory the customary dealer-to-factory order form, a copy of the police department's official purchase order, and the letter of explanation. Upon receipt of all the paperwork, Indian filed an application with the War Production Board. Once approved by the board, the factory notified the dealer of the expected date of shipment. Incidentally, the government allowed only 139 civilian passenger cars to be built in 1943 and another 610 in 1944. These were the only years in which America built more motorcycles than passenger cars.

Most noticeable of the Chief changes was the switch to the military-style unskirted fenders. This was in response to the government's edict that unnecessary material wouldn't be used for purely styling reasons. Also new was the handlebar crossbar, which was secured by a clip on each end. Color choices were changed to red, medium blue, navy blue, and gray, according to sales literature and observations of unrestored motorcycles. (The civilian Harleys were only available in silver or gray, at the factory's option.) The front fork was extended on the lower end to increase the rake.

To save costs, plating was minimized. On some Chiefs, the cylinders were painted black instead of nickel-plated. The horn face was the same as that used on the 1941 and 1942 Chiefs, but was black instead of chrome-plated. Likewise, black finish was applied to the instrument panel and the tank caps. On some motorcycles the following parts were Parkerized: wheel hubs, front fork spring leaves, front and rear brake plates, clutch pedal, brake pedal, and rear brake lever.

On the gearshift lever, a simple hole mated with the shift rod. Previously, the lever had a ball fitting that mated with the shift rod fitting. The shifter

During the war, Indian and Harley-Davidson sustained motorcycling enthusiasm with ads like this. Everyone looked forward to peacetime and to the return of motorcycling adventures.

rod had a right angle on each end, and the short section on each end was threaded to accept a nut. Before, the shifter rod was straight and threaded on each end to accept the ball fitting.

The primary-drive cover was given a reinforcing boss in the area around the top front bolt; this may have been introduced on some 1941 or 1942 Chiefs. On the generator belt guard, a clip was installed to secure the speedometer cable. The transmission cover had a reinforcement web; this was probably a running change during 1943. With the abandonment of fender skirts, the toolbox location had to be changed. The toolbox was mounted on the right side to the vertical rear fender brace above the chain guard and the rear springs using two P-shaped clips. Four small clips secured the taillight wire to the left side of the rear fender.

The following functional changes identified for the 1944 Chief are based on the 1944 parts book (some of these changes may have occurred between publication of the 1940 parts book and publication of the 1944 book). In the sump-valve group, the valve-disc spring and screen were different. New pistons were of a different alloy. A note of caution here: Beware of new-old-stock pistons and rings. As previously related by Allen Carter, Indian used parts made from recycled metal—melted-down pots and pans, in other words. Harley-Davidson had the same problem. Longtime Harley-Davidson dealer Tom Sifton recalled that for a while in the mid-1940s, police motorcycles got as little as 3,000 miles use on ring sets.

The Wartime Business Climate

The U.S. Army bought essentially all its motorcycles from Harley-Davidson, leaving to Indian the smaller job of supporting Allied armies. The rather dilapidated Wigwam played a role in the Army's decision, as Harley-Davidson's factory was in far better shape. It's one thing to promise large deliveries and another to make the deliveries.

Indian's main military motorcycle was the Model 741, a little twin of 30.50 cubic inches. Even though the U.S. Army opted for the 45-cubic-inch Harleys, Indian produced over 16,000 motorcycles, mostly 741s, in each of the business years 1942 and 1943. These went to British allies, whose military specifications called for substantial numbers of 30.50-cubic-inch (500-cc) side-valve motorcycles. In comparison, Harley-Davidson produced more than 29,000 military motorcycles in each of the same two years. Thus, in military business as in prewar civilian business, Springfield was locked into a one-third share. Still, a production rate of 16,000 motorcycles was well within the efficient realm of factory operations.

The business years of 1944 and 1945 were the Indian killers, with production levels of about 4,000 and 2,000, respectively. This meant layoffs, new hires, training, rehires, retraining, idle machinery, and significant nonmotorcycle subcontracts that had no benefit in posturing the Wigwam for the postwar motorcycle business. There was also the matter of large numbers of spare parts that the Wigwam had anticipated selling. Ultimately, the government prevailed in its assertion that these parts were not in the scope of the Indian contracts, which was a severe blow to Indian finances. Here's more on this from Indian staffer Allen Carter.

Why Indian Lost Money on Army Spare Parts, an Allen Carter Reminiscence

"One of the worst downfalls we had, was when the war was pretty much over. Joe Hosley had died. . . . Mr. du Pont brought up a guy named Burnstein, Doctor Burnstein.

"We used to have a guy named Doug Over-baugh. He had these big huge ledger books up in a special room. And he had one woman that worked for him, for years. . . . He had these huge ledger books; there must've been eight or ten of them, great big thick things with big sheets. He would open those up, and he could tell you where a certain part was in the plant, how many operations were on it. He always knew that. He watched, and he could tell by the cards the men turned in at nighttime where the part was, how many operations were on; he could tell you the whole thing.

"Well, somebody got the idea that was old-fashioned, and that they should bring in IBM and do this thing with an IBM setup. That was what really was the downfall of the company. Because they came in, and the first thing they did, they said, 'Well all these tools that you have spread around these machines, with numbers on them to make certain parts, they ought to be in one place.' When a guy gets an order to make something, he will call up someplace else and they'll bring up the tools for the machine. So they got rid of this thing of Doug Overbaugh's that had worked for years and years just perfectly. I could go down to Doug Overbaugh and say, Doug, where is so and so, and he would say, well just a minute. He would say, well it's down in Department 29, and he says right now it's got one more operation on it to finish it, or two, or three. That was great. You could do this in 5 minutes. He was on the second floor, down from where we were. And we'd go down there, and he could tell you right away. And if he wasn't there, there was a woman who worked for him.

"Well, once the IBM thing came in, then they decided to take all these tools all over the plant, all these special fixtures, and everything, and put them down in the cellar. And then they would issue the order to the guy in the cellar and he would pull the tools out to put on the different machines. Well, someplace along the line they didn't number these things right and they didn't fill the IBM cards out right, so they didn't know where in the hell they were. They had a whole cellar full, tons and tons of jigs and fixtures, but nobody—well some of it they could figure out, but the rest of it they couldn't.

"So when the war was over, we had about seven army contracts for various things. We were making parts for Boeing Aircraft and what-not like that. We were working for, what was it, 10 percent? Ten percent over cost, or something like that. We couldn't justify where we were on the cost of all these pieces in the plant. So they wouldn't pay us. I don't remember how many dollars were involved, but it was a hell of a lot of money that we could never justify because we couldn't show our cost sheets on it. . . . I think Indian got about one-third of the money that was due them. If [Indian] had left [the old ledgers] alone, they would've been all right.

"[Burnstein] was the guy that brought in IBM, and screwed it up really good. If they had just left everything alone, we would've been okay. On one contract, I know that we lost $600,000 on it because we couldn't justify the amount of work that was done on the thing. . . ."

Meanwhile, the Army had bought enough Harleys to enable Milwaukee to operate efficiently and to make healthy profits despite low markups dictated by the government. Indian couldn't win for losing.

Chapter 8

Last of the Wigwam Chiefs
1946–1948

Indian had new owners and new management after the war. In charge was young Ralph B. Rogers, who was something of a whiz-kid specializing in reviving sick companies. The significance to the Chief saga is that Rogers bought Indian to make a series of lightweight motorcycles, not to make Chiefs.

After over 25 years of competing with other Indian models, and usually being second or third banana in the publicity material, the Chief at last got top billing in 1946. But that wasn't an overt and well-deserved compliment. Instead, the company's poor financial status meant it could produce only the Chief in 1946. Here was belated, implied, but real recognition that the

Starting in 1947, the standard 110-mile-per-hour speedometer had a red bar painted across the odometer, and there was no trip meter. As an option, a speedometer with a trip meter was available. The ammeter had a pointer angled at 45 degrees to the right when in the neutral position; this was a running change incorporated on late-1946 Chiefs.

For 1946, the big deal was the new double-spring girder fork with a hydraulic shock absorber. Starting in 1946, the short inboard decorative aluminum strips used previously on the fenders were omitted. The Indian-head tank emblems were highlighted with translucent red. A small speedometer cable was fitted. Cylinders were black on 1946–1953 Chiefs. Jeff Hackett

This 1947 Chief is a Bonneville model featuring magneto ignition, high-lift cams, and polished ports. The 5.00x16-inch tires were standard (since late-1946); 4.50x18-inch tires were optional. All tires were labeled with Indian script. Although cosmetically restored, the engine had less than 400 original miles!

Chief had been the company's backbone all along, despite advertising policy that had favored other models for over a quarter of a century. When the going got tough and Indian could build only one model, it built its longtime sales leader, the Chief. The Chief had made most of the profits for a long time, profits that had sustained the other, less-popular tribesmen.

The headline feature for 1946 was the new girder front fork, which was a narrower version of the fork that had been used on the Model 841 shaft-drive Army motorcycle. Featuring two coil springs and a hydraulic shock absorber, the fork moved on four 4-inch-long links, two on the upper end of the steering head and two on the lower end. The fork was topped by different handlebars attached to risers mounted to the shock absorber. The steering head was 1 inch shorter, and the steering damper was built in.

Early-season models used leftover military Model 741 front wheels with small spokes and 4.50x18-inch tires; later Chiefs used regular wheels with small spokes and 5.00x16-inch tires. The front brake plate was polished on regular models but unpolished on police models. The fenders lacked the short decorative strips inboard of the full-length strips that had been fitted to earlier chiefs. All Chiefs had the front safety guard (standard in black); they had to because this is where the horn was mounted.

A running change was made to the instrument panel; late-1946 models had an ammeter with the pointer angled 45 degrees to the right (instead of straight up). On all 1946 Chiefs, a red bar was painted across the main odometer section.

The saddle was equipped with side-plate protectors; previously, these protectors had been fitted to military and police models only. Also, the front saddle connection was heavier. The exhaust headers were mounted to the frame by a low bracket instead of being mounted to the cylinders. The headers were one piece and the mounting hardware

Sometime during the 1947 production year, the old-style cam case cover (without wraparound) was reintroduced. A new oil pump was introduced for 1947. It's thicker and more angular, and had no small boss (protrusion) at the 10 o'clock position. The 1947 Chief was offered in three levels of trim. With the accessories of De Luxe solo saddle and chrome front and rear safety guards, the motorcycle was designated a "Sportsman." Note the chain guard, which doesn't completely encircle the kickstarter; this guard made its debut on the late-1946 Chiefs.

formerly used in the footboard area was omitted. The right footboard bracket was routed over the top of the exhaust pipe instead of under it. On early-1946 models, the kickstarter was black; later models had a cadmium-plated starter.

Early-1946 Chiefs had the kickstarter completely encircled by the chain guard, as before, but late-1946 Chiefs didn't have the kickstarter completely encircled (see illustration). On the center stand, the latch was removed and replaced by a flat-strip

This 1947 Seafoam Blue Chief was a hybrid featuring the Clubman solo saddle and the Sportsman/Roadmaster chrome safety guards. Chrome-plated rear fender braces and chrome pedals were popular with riders, but these were standard in black. On 1946–1948 Chiefs the generator belt guard was color matched to the tanks and fenders. The motorcycle was restored by American Indian Specialists.

spring. The center stand also had longer legs. The longer stand meant the Chief was lifted higher, which was necessary in order to maintain stability with the longer front fork.

The generator belt guard was painted the same color as the tanks, fenders, and chain guard (instead of black). The generator belt guard shield, introduced on 1940 Chiefs, was continued, but there was no circular fuse block on the top of the shield. The toolbox was changed in order to accommodate the small-diameter speedometer cable. On the rear brake, the actuating lever was cadmium-plated instead of black. The lever and shaft were serrated; earlier arms had a D-shaped hole that interfaced with a D-shaped shaft. The support casting on the shock absorber for the rear axle had a reinforcing rib cast along the upper surface, as on military models; previously, the reinforcement was welded. The tailpipe clamp consisted of a circular clip around the pipe, a rubber bushing, a P-shaped clip with the bushing in the large end and a bolt

through the small end and the rear fender, plus another bolt through the bushing and two nuts. This was an excellent shock-absorbing clamp that eliminated the cracking that occurred with the earlier one-piece P-shaped clamp. Unfortunately, the clamp was used on the 1946 and 1947 Chiefs only.

1947 Chief Refinements

Styling was the keynote of the 1947 models. The front-fender running light was changed to the Indian-head-and-war-bonnet design. The front safety (crash) guard was standard issue in black. Gas-tank emblems were changed for the second year in a row. The indian-head emblems used in 1946 were replaced for 1947 by a chrome-plated emblem consisting of the word *Indian* in script. This script tank emblem was used from 1947 through the end of Chief production in 1953 (although a decal was used around the emblem for 1952 and 1953.) To form the basis of a so-called three-model line-up, three accessory packages were offered that produced the stripped-down Clubman, the modestly accessorized Sportsman, and the all-out full-dresser Roadmaster. See the Appendix for details.

The operating lever on the front brake's plate was cadmium-plated. The front-brake cable attachment on the operating lever was achieved by simply twisting the cable under a compressing washer, so there was no straight-through action and the cable would flex when the brake was applied. The links on the front fork were longer, 4 1/2 inches instead of 4 inches.

On late-1947 models, the side stand was longer and was mounted forward on the frame. This feature debuted officially the following year. On the generator, a voltage regulator was standard, and the generator cutout relay was no longer available.

There was no generator-belt-guard shield. Mentioned earlier as a running change on late-1946 Chiefs, the chain guard with partial kickstarter coverage was official throughout the year. The generator belt guard had no hole for oiling the generator.

For 1947 only, a larger cast-iron plunger-style oil pump was fitted. The pump was thicker and had a more square shape and, in fact, resembled the aluminum gear pump of 1948 and later. For the first time since 1934, a four-speed transmission wasn't offered.

Planning for a Better Chief

Indian needed a better Chief to compete with the Harley-Davidson 74-cubic-inch overheads that had been introduced in 1941. On September 30, 1947, Indian President Ralph Rogers submitted a

The streamlined skirted-fender sidecar was first offered in the 1940 line-up. ©Hans Halberstadt

report of the board of directors that included the following assessment of the Chief: "Model 349: It has been suggested that the heavy-duty motorcycle not be dropped at this particular time and that thought be given to the manufacture of a Model 349, essentially a further improvement on our present 74 cu. inch machine. Our principal disadvantage is the inability of our 74 cu. inch machine to stay with the 74" overhead valve model produced by Harley-Davidson. We are going to determine whether we can increase the stroke of the present 74 cu. inch flat head engine to make it an 80 cu. inch machine and in that way overcome this disad-

The rider was Bill Meador, who had just won the 1947 Southwestern TT Championship in Waco, Texas. This was one of the last TT victories for a Chief, as British motorcycles were soon to dominate the tight and twisty courses. Clyde Earl

The new-for-1948 front-wheel-driven speedometer and aluminum gear-driven oil pump stand out. The front fork had a grease fitting in the top middle. Also shown here is the 1948 horn, which had a different face. On 1946–1951 Chiefs the horn was mounted to the front safety guard as shown here, so the guard was standard equipment (some were black). On the rear fender of this machine are luggage tie-down bars, a period accessory.

vantage. If that can be done and tests out satisfactorily, it might then be possible by improving the clutch and using a cushion sprocket to manufacture heavy-duty machines without too great an investment in tools and tooling."

1948: Last of the Wigwam Chiefs

Starting in 1948, the front tire was available only in the 5.00x16-inch size. The front-brake backing plate had a built-in speedometer drive. The wheel hub had an angled grease fitting. The front fork had Zerk grease fittings to lubricate the bushings. Sport handlebars were optional. These were the same height as the standard bars but narrower. The sport handlebars were the same as those used on the Model 648 Daytona Sport Scout.

Several running changes were implemented during the year's production run. On the right crankcase, a cast-in flywheel scraper replaced the sump valve, so the sump-valve plate was omitted from the lower part of the case. The frame's upper rear fork crossbar was changed from a tubular to rectangular cross section. A longer side stand was mounted farther forward (this had been a running change on late-1947 Chiefs). Although the scraper and crossbar were advertised as 1948 improvements, some production models didn't have one or both of these features. The hand shifter mount (under the forward edge of tanks) was a welded tube instead of a casting. At least two authentic 1948 Chiefs have surfaced with the old-style tubular crossbar but with the new-style gearshift-lever mount previously discussed.

Most Chief history was lived anonymously by countless riders who roamed the highways. Springfield Indian dealer Fritzie Baer shakes hands with the tourist. Neither bungee cords nor fiberglass tote boxes were around back then, so riders tied ropes around bundles carried on top of the rear fender. Informal riding clothes replaced the prewar uniforms. Butch Baer collection

In June 1948, Max Bubeck rode this Chase/Bubeck "Chout" to a top speed of 135.58 miles per hour during the Rosamond (California) Dry Lake speed trials. The one-way run, which was bothered by a slight crosswind, was the all-time fastest for an unstreamlined Indian. The Chout consisted of a Chief engine in a 101 Scout frame. Both cylinders had reshaped inlet ports to accommodate twin carburetors. A high-gear-only transmission reduced drag. Max Bubeck

On the right side of the engine was the new aluminum oil pump with a flat outer surface. This was a five-gear pump featuring a triple-gear supply section and a double-gear return section. The exhaust system construction was different. The front and rear headers were built as one piece, and the header connected to the muffler/tailpipe assembly beneath the kickstarter. The generator was equipped with a voltage regulator instead of a cutout. A silent ball-lock kickstarter was fitted. A step backward was the simple one-piece P-shaped tailpipe clamp, which replaced the 1946–1947 five-piece shock-absorbing clamp.

The 1948 Chiefs were the last Indians produced in the historic Wigwam on State Street. Future Indian production would be on the other side of town, in one-story buildings deemed more acceptable for mass production of the forthcoming European-styled lightweight singles and vertical twins.

The 1948 Sales Pitch

How did Indian dealers convince potential buyers that the side-valve Chief wasn't inherently inferior to the overhead-valve Harley Seventy-fours and Sixty-ones? Simple; they just turned the customers' attention to the automobile world. Side-

The Chief was forever playing second (or third) fiddle to other Indian models such as this 1949 Arrow 13-cubic-inch (220-cc) single. In the immediate postwar era, Indian spent more than $600,000 developing a line of modular singles, twins, and an in-line four (never produced). Engineering and manufacturing capabilities were so strapped that Indian dropped the Chief from the 1949 line-up. The Wigwam never recovered. The rider is actress Jane Russell. Jimmy Hill collection

valve Fords had been the favorites of the hot-rod world for over a decade. The side-valve Plymouth was then a big seller of the Chrysler corporation, as was the side-valve Studebaker, which was making serious inroads against Ford and Chevrolet. Side-valve engines were the accepted standard in other words. But the clinching argument often came from the General Motors stable. On the low end of the line GM offered the overhead-valve Chevrolet, and on the top end of the line the company offered a side-valve Cadillac. Case closed.

The Chase/Bubeck "Chout"

Prior to the war, rider/tuner Frank Christian had made an impact on the Southern California scene with his 80-cubic-inch (1,300-cc) stroker

Chief. Christian had used the Z Metal flywheels of mid-1938 and later, plus British-made Hepolite aluminum-alloy pistons. These features had turned the stroker Chief into a reliable road concept, whereas before such strokers (including the 1933 Alzina special) had led short lives between blow-ups and wear-outs. Christian's friends Frank Chase and Max Bubeck took up the stroker cause and at a number of speed trials got faster and faster speeds from their stroker Chief.

Their efforts culminated in June 1948 when Bubeck, the smaller of the pair, rode the Chase/Bubeck "Chout" to an all-time high speed for an unstreamlined Indian, 135.58 miles per hour. This was a one-way run, as always in Southern California, because the large number of riders

In late-1949, at the request of Indian President Ralph Rogers, the Vincent HRD motorcycle company of England installed a 61-cubic-inch (1,000-cc) Vincent engine in a Chief frame. The mildly tuned Rapide engine configuration was used rather than the faster Black Shadow variant. Even with the touring engine, the motorcycle easily topped 100 miles per hour. No production versions were built, however. Peter Arundel collection

took too much time to run the bikes both ways. The "Chout" name came from the combination of the Chief engine in the frame of a 101 Scout. Although the twin-carburetor Chout was equipped with an oxygen bottle, Bubeck didn't use oxygen injection for fear of a blowup. Among the more important tuning steps was the care taken to achieve precise ignition timing; stock Chiefs usually had one-cylinder firing way off the mark when the other cylinder was spot on. In winning the Rosamond Dry Lake speed trial, the Chout bettered the best 80-cubic-inch Harley-Davidson Knucklehead, in a classic replay of the old bumble-bee fable. You know the story. The bumble bee, not realizing it theoretically can't fly, goes ahead and flies anyway. The Chout was a flyer.

The Chief Is Jilted

Meanwhile, in the summer of 1948, the time came to begin building next year's Chiefs. But the Chief was jilted. Chiefs weren't produced because all the company's resources were instead dedicated to bringing the new lightweight singles and twins into production.

President Rogers had his hands full, trying to get the 1949 lightweight line-up ready. Engineering and subcontracting problems were turning Rogers' dream into a nightmare. Deliveries were behind schedule, and the lightweights weren't reliable. The only thing going right was Rogers' masterfully orchestrated publicity campaign that featured movie stars and famous athletes. Among the

Here's another one that never made it. Indian envisioned this 1949 Chief with a foot shift and hand clutch; however, only a few prototypes were completed before all Chief production was halted. Dealers who had been promised a foot-shift Chief were given the option of canceling their orders. The buddy seat was the same one available as an accessory for the vertical twins and singles, except that the Chief seat had spring suspension. Emmett Moore

endorsers were Alan Ladd, Robert Ryan, Jane Russell, band leader Vaughn Monroe, Notre Dame quarterback Johnny Lujack, and Cleveland Indians pitcher Bob Feller.

But the Rogers strategy met an insurmountable object in September 1948 when the British government devalued the pound sterling by about 25 percent. This lowered the prices of comparable English lightweights by about the same amount and forced Rogers into an alignment with the English firm of Brockhouse. Though it wasn't yet completely clear, Indian was entering what chess players call the end game. Every move from this point on could only delay the inevitable defeat of Indian as an American motorcycle manufacturer.

Chapter 9

The Twilight Years
1949–1953

The Chief wasn't mass-produced for the 1949 season due to production difficulties with the lightweight 1949 Arrow single and Scout vertical twin. Only a handful of prototype Chiefs were built with hand clutch and foot shift. One was photographed at the El Paso, Texas, dealership.

Falling Behind in the Technical Race

Although the Chief performed adequately as a luxury touring motorcycle, by 1949 the model was falling ever more out of fashion. For this reason, an interesting prototype Chief was developed in 1949. In Indian President Ralph Rogers' January 20, 1949, report to the

A typical rider's view of a 1950–1953 Chief. Because the front forks were 3 inches longer, the saddle height was increased about 2 inches—solo seat versus solo seat, buddy seat versus buddy seat. Even with the lower solo saddle, a 5-foot, 9-inch rider can barely plant both feet flat on the ground.

The 1952–1953 fork shield is shown. The black lower fork legs and black generator belt guard are correct for 1950–1953 Chiefs. The 1952–1953 front safety guard was poorly mounted by a single through-bolt, instead of by two clamps through a welded-on mounting plate. John Bull rubber tie-down straps replaced metal clips for routing some wiring and tubing. Two were on the left front down tube. Jeff Hackett

This 1951 Chief shows off the telescopic front fork intro-duced a year earlier. The other big news from 1950 was the 80-cubic-inch (1,300-cc) engine, achieved by a longer stroke. The front fender had a new shape with slightly smaller skirts. The bulge on the front of the primary-drive case houses the "Torque Evener" sprocket, a spring-loaded shock absorber that produced smoother low-speed running

board of directors, he tells the story: "There is an ever-increasing demand for assurance that we are not going out of the 'big' motorcycle business. Dealers insist that we have a program to compete with the 74 OHV Harley. Along these lines, we are just completing negotiations with the Vincent HRD Rapide Company in England to install in a Model 348 and in a Model 349 motorcycle their 1000cc overhead-valve V-twin engine and transmis-sion. . . . It might be possible for us to furnish this motorcycle in time for the spring of 1950."

As related by Phil Vincent in Roy Harper's *The Vincent HRD Story*, the Chief arrived at the Vincent factory in England in late August, and within a few weeks the prototype was completed and road test-ed. The "Vindian" was shipped to Springfield, but no orders were forthcoming because, according to Vincent, Indian decided the regular Vincent motor-cycles were a better sales proposition.

Vincent's recollections, as related in Harper's book, are inaccurate on one point. Vincent stated that the Vincent engine fit nicely into the Chief frame, with only a single modification, that being the removal of most of the rear down tube (be-neath the saddle). A Vindian was constructed for Australian Peter Arundel in 1996. Arundel learned, and has the in-process photos to prove it, that the

Vincent engine won't fit beneath the horizontal frame tube just below the tanks. On the Arundel Vindian, it was necessary to completely remove the standard Indian tube and replace it with a Harley-style tube that angled upward from the steering head to the midpoint of the top frame tube. The original Vindian was doubtless built the same way. Indeed, close examination confirms that the 1949 Vindian didn't have the regular In-dian upper frame tube.

From the minutes of the board of directors meeting for April 14, 1949, we find the following: "After discussion, it was decided in view of the vari-ous conditions . . . including . . . evidence that the Vincent engine would prove satisfactory from the standpoint of installation and operation, definitive action on this agreement be postponed to a later

The correct Indian Chum-Me seat had a more squared-off nose than Harley buddy seats of the era. The short thick fringes were correct; most restorations include longer and thinner fringes. Indian supplied some saddles with black handrails and others with chrome handrails. The accessory aluminum luggage rack was phased in dur-ing the late 1940s.

The 1950 and 1951 Chiefs appear identical. The front and rear exhaust headers were built as one piece, and the header connects to the muffler/tailpipe assembly beneath the kickstarter. The windshield shown is the best available in terms of mimicking the original design

In this 1951 shot, we see New York City police officers training a new recruit at Randall's Island. Note the 1936 gearshift lever on this 1948 Chief. Some departments opted for older equipment. For example, Yonkers, New York, preferred the older shifter. In other cases individual officers might select prior-year features. The rear-wheel-driven speedometer was standard on police Indians. Rich Carrano collection

date." In conclusion, it appears that a factor in Indian's refusal to mass produce the Vindian was the incompatibility of the engine and frame. Indian's failing economic health was undoubtedly also a factor in this stillborn idea.

1950: Top Dog Too Late

By 1950, the planned-for lightweight Indian motorcycle revolution had already failed. Mom and pop, and brother and sister, weren't going to sign up for motorcycling despite all those movie star and professional athletes endorsing the new lightweight Indian singles and vertical twins. The company was now critically ill. In January, Rogers was forced out and Brockhouse took over.

As in 1946, the Chief's stature as the company's main moneymaker was again reinforced in the 1950 line-up. The big V-twin returned after a one-year absence. The Chief was top dog too late because the new Brockhouse management shared Rogers' disinterest in Chief production. The mini-factory was kept in operation to gather meager profits but mainly to present the appearance of resumed large-scale production. This was to strengthen Brockhouse's real goal, control of the large network of Indian dealers.

The headline features were the new telescopic front fork and the 80-cubic-inch (1,300-cc) engine.

The enlarged displacement of the Eighty was achieved by increasing the stroke from 4 7/16 inches to 4 13/16 inches, while holding the bore at 3 1/4 inches. To allow for the longer stroke, the cylinder heads were recessed 3/16 inch and the piston skirts were shorter. Smoother low-speed running was achieved by providing a "Torque Evener" engine sprocket for the primary chain. This was an engine shock absorber in which a coil spring was alternately loaded and unloaded.

The front fender had a shorter front section and a smaller skirt. The fork had black upper and lower legs. Some 1950 Chiefs were equipped with a rear-wheel-driven speedometer; these were probably police models using the old Corbin speedometer head unit. Most 1950 Chiefs were fitted with a Stewart-Warner speedometer that was driven off the front wheel. On the frame's right front down tube, a hole accepted the oil tank breather tube. The shifter mount under the forward section of the tanks was welded on instead of cast in (this had been a running change during the 1948 season). On the tanks, the Indian script was trimmed with red background paint along the edges of the lettering. To account for the taller parking stance resulting from the telescopic fork, the side stand mounting angle was changed. The twist-to-lock Raceway air cleaner (without a center-mounting screw) became a standard item. On the forward part of the primary-drive cover was a bulge to allow clearance for the "Torque Evener" shock absorber. Raised aluminum passenger footboard extenders replaced the earlier iron horizontal fittings.

Said the headline in the June 1951 *Cycle* magazine, "If You're Looking For Power, An Indian Packs the Most of All—80 Inches." The tester, Officer Filker of the Alhambra Police Department, remarked: "To motorcyclists the world over, America is recognized as the land of big twins, and the flowing tribal headdress of the American Indian has long been significant of one of this country's most impressive models, the Indian Chief. . . .

"The current [adaptation] of a cushion primary drive made riding in heavy traffic much more enjoyable than might be imagined. Power impulses of the big twin, when idling along in high gear, were very smooth because of the torque evener. What with its brute strength, a three speed transmission works out very well on the Chief, although it was the rider's opinion that a four-speed box with a wider range of gearing would be even more suitable. Added weight when riding double makes almost no change in the bike's handling or acceleration, and this particular

This 1953 Chief has the rare original 4.75x16-inch Dunlop Gold Seal tires. Indian introduced these to lower the saddle height, which had climbed because of the longer front end. The muffler was the same as that used on the Indian vertical twins. The low exhaust routing leaves room for larger saddlebags, but oil flung from the chain rapidly covers the exhaust system. Chrome caps were an extra-cost alternative to standard painted caps for 1952 and 1953.

model should make an excellent sidecar partner. Cruising speeds at 60 to 65 miles per hour averaged 40 miles to the gallon of gas. At this clip the powerful 80 incher had just barely gone to work, and the vibration was at a minimum."

Filker, however, wasn't a fan of the wet clutch, long an item of controversy. He wrote, "One feature that has been retained through the years and may bear a second look is the Chief's oil clutch. Until the operator has become adept through practice, engagement of low gear without clashing is difficult, and considerable drag was noticed when shifting all gears."

1951: Refinements

On the tanks, Indian script with a black background was phased in; the 1950-style script with a red background was continued until the supply was depleted. A new, higher clutch-pedal mount was achieved by welding a tube on top of the casting formerly used for this purpose; this was to accommodate the clutch brake.

Some late-1951 Chiefs were fitted with rear-drive Corbin speedometers. These had white markings and a white non-arrow pointer over a black base. Other details of the late-1951 Corbin units are uncertain, because either one or both of the types observed on both 1952 and 1953 Chiefs was used. It's unclear as to which came first, and for that matter, it's possible that the factory used a "salt-and-pepper" random use of both types concurrently over the years. These two speedometer possibilities were a BSC-labeled unit with 5-mile-per-hour increments and a non-BSC-labeled unit with 2-mile-per-hour increments. Since the new Corbin units had a smaller diameter than the Stewart-Warner units used previously, a bezel was added to fill the gap between the speedometer and the speedometer hole. According to the parts book, a new rear fender applied throughout 1951. This suggests that the factory at one point believed the rear-drive speedometers would predominate. Those machines fitted with the rear-drive Corbin unit with the

The Chief Versus Harley-Davidson Panheads

Cycle magazine's road tests of the 1950 Chief, the 1950 Harley Sixty-one, and the 1952 Harley Seventy-four show that the Chief had acceleration comparable to the Harley Sixty-one but inferior to the Harley Seventy-four. The Chief accelerated from a standing start to 40 miles per hour in 6 seconds; the Harley Sixty-one took 4 seconds for this feat. From 40 miles per hour in second gear to 80 miles per hour in third (high) gear the Chief required 16 seconds; the Harley Sixty-one also needed 16 seconds to do the same thing. My interpretation of the data says that in a high-gear-only roll-on contest, the Chief had the edge on the Harley Sixty-one. But it certainly wasn't a chore to downshift the Sixty-one to third, where it was equal to the Chief.

Comparisons with the Harley Seventy-four are a little muddled because different statistics were used by Cycle in 1952 (1/10- and 1/4-mile drags instead of 0 to 40, 0 to 60, and so on). One statistic for the 1950 Chief and the 1952 Harley Seventy-four was common to each road test: top speed. The Chief managed 92 miles per hour and the Harley 102.88 miles per hour. The Harley was handicapped by a loose surface on the dry lake course, however, as evidenced by its ability to top out at an even 100 miles per hour in third gear, less than 3 miles per hour slower than top speed in fourth. My interpretation of the data says that the Harley Seventy-four had more soup than the Chief in a high-gear roll-on contest and that the Harley in third gear would walk off from the Chief. This is hardly surprising, as the Harley-Davidson Seventy-four Panhead could run with or outrun any motorcycle commonly available at the time, the exception being the expensive and seldom-seen English-built Vincent Black Shadow, powered by a 61-cubic-inch V-twin engine.

Despite the statistics, one informal data point sticks in my mind. I listened to the last Los Angeles policeman who rode a Chief on patrol, a guy who stuck with his Indian more than a year after the rest of the force converted to the Milwaukee brand. He swore the Chief had more get up and go than the Harleys. The wide gap between second and third (high) on the Chief meant you could really feel the torque as the Chief accelerated in a high-gear roll-on. Maybe the Chief just felt stronger than the Panheads. Got another theory?

black-and-white face had a plug in the hole in the front brake's backing plate formerly used for the speedometer's front-drive mechanism.

1952–1953: The Last of the Tribe

For 1952 the Chief was restyled. The most obvious changes to the final Chiefs were the new front fender, front-fork upper panel, engine cowling, and a low-level chaase system. The front fender was smaller, having a shorter arc and a smaller skirt.

On the handlebars were external, English-style throttle, choke, and ignition controls. Gone from the left bar was the dimmer switch, which was relocated car style to the left footboard. The speedometer running change begun on late-1951 Chiefs applied to all 1952 Chiefs. The instrument panel included a Corbin speedometer and mounting bezel as described earlier for some 1951 models.

On nonpolice models, the engine breathed through an Amal carburetor. Although the advertising ballyhoo counted this as an improvement, the fact was that Indian couldn't afford a small order of Linkert units. The Amal carburetors earned a reputation for starting fires, and I've witnessed one of these flame-ups. Police models still got Linkert carburetors. The cylinder heads were milled to increase the compression ratio, and each was fitted with a brass plug to secure the spark-plug insert.

The new safety-guard didn't have a mounting plate. Consequently, the horn couldn't be mounted to the guard. Instead, the horn was secured to a bracket that hung from the lower end of the steering head.

The compression ratio was increased to 6.7:1 by milling the heads. Also the combustion chambers roof had a different slope that further reduced volume and increased the compression ratio. To prevent the 18 cylinder head bolts from bottoming out, 7/16-inch flat washers were used.

The transmission and primary drives had independent oil baths, so the transmission case had a boss drilled and tapped for oil level and didn't have two communicating holes to connect with the primary-drive case. The center stand had an offset L-shape to the legs, which provided an over-center action.

In order to accommodate an optional larger police battery, the inner edges of the lower left and right frame tubes were flattened, thus providing the required extra width. The battery tray was welded in place instead of being removable. Also related to the optional larger battery was the different rear fender. Of the same general appearance as earlier Chief skirted rear fenders, the fender was flattened

Indian advertising said the 1952–1953 engine cowling mimics the crankcase of the Vincent V-twin sold by Indian dealers. To clear the cowling, the rear exhaust header pipe was bent in a different arc. The kickstarter was encircled by a removable piece of the lower chain guard. This bike was restored by Starklite Cycle.

across the front. On the frame, there was no serial number on the left rear lower "wraparound" of the rear springs. Instead, the serial number was on the right front footboard mount.

Changes on 1953 models were minor. Occasionally, riders of the 1952 Chiefs reported the front fender fouling the horn (beneath the steering head) on steep bumps. This was cured by placing the fender-mounting tabs 1/2-inch lower on the fork legs, which gave the fender an additional 1/2-inch clearance to the horn. Late 1953 Chiefs had a longer kick-start lever. The front axel on late 1953 Chiefs was nitrided (black finish) instead of cadmium-plated.

Indian Chief Versus Harley-Davidson Big-Twin Development

Chiefs were in production for the 1922 through 1953 sales seasons. Without the impact of World War II, that would've been 32 seasons. All of the 1943 through 1945 Chiefs were basically built to one specification as the Model 344, with only minor differences in military and civilian versions. In other words, wartime development was essentially halted by government edict. So, counting the war years of 1943–1945 as one season equates to 30 model years of Chief production.

Of the 30 Chief seasons, 15 saw significant technical changes and 15 didn't. There were four extended periods without noteworthy technical changes. These were the 1922–1925, 1928–1930,

1942–1944, and 1951–1953 seasons. In the first nine Chief production years of 1922–1930, only two years, 1926 and 1927, saw the introduction of important technical changes. This accounted for the gradual drop in Chief popularity compared to the Harley-Davidson big twins, a situation attacked by the new president, E. Paul du Pont, with the 1931 models.

The biggest burst of Chief engineering activity occurred on the 1931–1940 models, in which only a single year, 1937, saw the absence of important technical changes. But because of the continuing decline of the company's financial health, and later the internal rivalry between the Chief and the postwar lightweights, the 1941–1953 era saw relatively few technical advances.

Meanwhile, as detailed in the author's book *Inside Harley-Davidson* (also published by Motorbooks International), Harley-Davidson's big-twin engineering efforts from the post-1922 era were much more substantial than Indian's. Milwaukee's years of minimal technical changes were 1927, 1929, 1933, 1942, "military season," 1946, 1947, and 1950. So Harley-Davidson's 30 comparable seasons of 1922–1953 saw 22 seasons with noteworthy technical changes (compared to Indian's 15) and 8 seasons without noteworthy technical changes (compared to Indian's 15).

In summary, the Indian Chief suffered two periods of engineering inactivity, the 1922–1930 and 1941–1953 eras. The earlier quiet period was one of neglect (1922–1926) and concentration on the newly acquired Four (1927–1930). The 1941–1953 engineering slowdown was the result of the company's declining financial strength and concentration of engineering effort on the ultimately unsuccessful lightweight overhead-valve singles and vertical twins. Paralleling Indian's on-again off-again Chief engineering history was Harley-Davidson's basically continuous big-twin engineering program.

No Substitute for Cubic Inches?

Over the years, the Indian Chief has been criticized as an example of continued obsolescence. From a performance standpoint, the criticism is invalid. The later Indian Chiefs weren't trendy in a technological sense, that's for sure. But untrendy and obsolete are two different things.

Right up to the last, the Chiefs were built for the open road and for long straight-ahead running. Name me one "modern" 650-cc British vertical twin of the era that could cruise on the open road as fast and for as long as the Chief and with as much comfort. I might be willing to call the

The 1952–1953 front fender was smaller than the 1950–1951 fender. The horn was secured to a bracket hung from the steering head. On the footboard was the dimmer switch. The bench-style passenger seat lowered the saddle about 1 1/2 inches from the 1950–1951 level. The solo saddle remained optional for the last two years of Chief production. The Raceway air cleaner, previously an accessory, was standard for 1952 and 1953. This motorcycle was restored by Starklite Cycle. © Hans Halberstadt

contest a rough draw. Might. As to the classic Indian-versus-Harley scenario, for smooth running and comfort I'll pick a 1950s Indian Chief any day of the week over a rigid-frame Harley Panhead.

What really gets to the critics is the fact that Indian got away with a lot of 1920s technology, plus a few improvements, and got away with the trick into the 1950s. The Indian Chief stands out as a sort of cousin to the flathead Fords, soldiering on and succeeding despite bucking the overhead-valve trend.

Many have said that the Harley-Davidson KR series side-valve racers of the mid-1950s and 1960s were a triumph of development over design. The Chiefs were the opposite: triumphs of design over development. What worked in 1922 worked in 1953, and if you wanted to chase the sun from Phoenix to Los Angeles in 1953 and chase it on two wheels, only two motorcycles bettered the Chief. These were the BMW-opposed twins and the prohibitively expensive British-built Vincents. Harleys, Triumphs, BSAs, and the rest didn't do the job any better.

Ready for the Age of Freeways and Interstates

The October 1952 *Cycle* magazine has a picture that keeps coming into my mind. The picture isn't of an Indian. What we see is editor Bob Greene riding an Ariel (British) 500-cc single-cylinder sports model into a sweeping left-hand curve. So why have I remembered this shot for more than 40 years? Because the caption says profoundly more now than it did then: "Peeling rubber (off the footpegs, that is) on the beautiful, new, yet unused, Los Angeles freeway clover leaf. . . ." Los Angeles had only one freeway at that point, but the freeway explosion was at hand and along with it, the explosion of interstate highways. Somehow, through decades of highway improvement and ever-faster motorcyclists, the Indian factory had kept the Chief in the game. The Indian Chief was a better motorcycle than perhaps it should have been, a motorcycle that was good enough on the open road to be competitive over the next decade. But it was not to be.

1950–1953 Production

In the final four production years, 1950 through 1953, Chiefs were built in the Myrick Building in downtown Springfield. The old State Street Wigwam was used for storage and shipping only. In 1952 and 1953, the company house organ, *Pow Wow*, emphasized the line of British motorcycles now being sold by Indian dealers. These included AJS, Matchless, James, Norton, Royal Enfield, and Vincent.

But *Pow Wow* also included publicity photos of Chief production scenes, giving the impression that Chief production had a high priority with the British-dominated "The Indian Company."

Said Indian staffer Emmett Moore, "We were in the process of bamboozling the dealers as to the future Indian plans. We didn't want to admit that there weren't anymore Indians, and we kept the dealers strung along with stories of production later on. Anytime there were machines sitting around like that, Bob [Finn] would go around and take pictures of them to back up the story."

The photos showed only five workers in the engine shop and five on the final assembly line. Production of roughly 500 Chiefs annually amounted to a token effort of less than 10 percent of previous so-so years' production levels. From evidence here and there, it appears that the 2,000 or so 1950–1953 Chiefs were assembled from stocks left over after the last big run of Chiefs, 1948 models assembled at the Wigwam.

December 1953, Curtain Call

From a December 2, 1953, letter to all dealers:

"AN IMPORTANT MESSAGE TO ALL DEALERS: The management of the Indian Company has just completed a study of conditions adversely affecting motorcycle production in the United States. This has led to a decision to suspend assembly of complete motorcycles at Springfield during 1954. The sole purpose of this production holiday is to strengthen the position of the Company for future activities in the motorcycle manufacturing field. During this period, Indian manufacturing facilities will be engaged in parts fabrication and other revenue producing operations.

"An intact and aggressive organization is prepared for action as the United States Distributor for the top ranking British built motorcycles. Along with our Indian Brave and Papoose, such famous names as Norton, Vincent, Royal Enfield, A.J.S. and Matchless round out the complete 1954 motorcycle program.

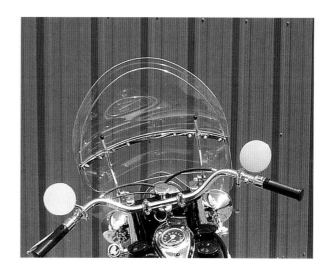

Late-1951, 1952, and 1953 Chiefs were fitted with a white-on-black 110-mile-per-hour speedometer, some with the "BSC" label and others without. The painted tank caps were stock.

"This program, which will be energetically promoted, is realistic and will make money for every participating dealer. We urge your continued loyal support."

Sketchy records indicate that 500 Chiefs were manufactured in each of the last four years, 1950 through 1953. But motor numbers suggest 800 1953 models were built. It's also possible that Indian skipped some numbers. Whatever the exact number, the production of telescopic Chiefs was trivial when compared to the explosive growth of motorcycling as a whole, a growth fueled by the British motorcycle invasion. The Indian organization, without the Indian factory, survived until 1959 as the importer of Indian-labeled English-built Royal Enfields, and from 1960 through mid-1962 as the "Matchless Indian" company, which imported English-built Matchless motorcycles.

Alongside survived the Indian dealers. Some kept at it for as long as they could with an Indian sign out front; others took on other motorcycle lines before the final Indian collapse. A few were lucky enough to hang on until the next revolution in American motorcycling, the Japanese invasion of the 1960s. Today, there are still a few motorcycle dealerships whose roots reach back to the happy days of the Indian Chief.

Chapter 10

Indian Fun

In the Indian-versus-Harley days, any large town had only two motorcycle shops, and each shop had its own formal club and its own informal society. People who rode Indians didn't mingle much with people who rode Harleys, and vice-versa. The two groups didn't dislike each other, at least not anymore than Dallas Cowboys fans and San Francisco Forty-Niners fans disliked each other. Away from motorcycling they got along fine, but if you were an ardent motorcyclist, you bonded with the riders you knew best, and those were the riders of your brand. As time wore on, the Indian riders learned that some of their riding friends shared mutual nonmotorcycling interests. In other cases, as riding days dwindled, Indian fans developed new interests together. They had been friends centered in motorcycling, and

Many of today's Indians are restored with practical updates to later specifications. These are "rider" bikes as opposed to "show" bikes. This 1934 Chief has a 1939–1946 oil pump and distributor drive. Optional aluminum cylinder heads of this style were unique to 1934. © Hans Halberstadt

The owner of this "rider" has opted for practical changes, including black cylinders and the rider-designed sprung passenger seat. A 1941–1942 horn fitted—why not, it works. The bike was photographed on a Colorado road run. The restoration was done by Mike Steckley of Vintage Motorcycles.

In this circa 1955 shot, how fitting that Howard Mitzell hill-climbs his Chief into the sunset, in the twilight years of the Indian Company. Howard Mitzell was a champion climber from the early 1930s through the 1950s. Chiefs were highly competitive hill-climbers into the 1960s. Chuck Myles

Indian wins again! The year was 1989. Chuck Myles, Indian dealer from Sloansville, New York, preps his updated ex-Tom Paradise hill-climber—the same one campaigned by Howard Mitzell 40 years earlier. Looking on was Butch Baer, son of former Springfield dealer Fritzie Baer. Ten minutes after the photo, Myles finished second in the New England Sportsman (amateur) Hillclimb Championships. He beat every late-model Harley entered. Myles still campaigns this ancient warrior. Chuck Myles collection

they wanted to stay friends after the ball game was over. So among Indian's legacies are lifelong friendships of people who used to gather at the Indian shops more than half a century ago. These are the last of the original tribe. To move among them is a high privilege for any motorcyclist too young to have ridden a brand-new Indian.

Beyond the ever smaller cluster of yesterday's throttle twisters, the Indian movement is sustained by younger people. A few, like me, were awestruck when we were six or eight or ten years old, and upon seeing those elegant motorcycles in the everyday scene, vowed someday to have an Indian. But most of today's Indian riders have caught the magic entirely within the antique-motorcycle movement.

Mainly, I think, Indian motorcycles capture hearts because of Indian styling and the Indian saga. In the 1960s, the brash Japanese took over the world of motorcycling. They did this not only with a well-reasoned disregard of old engineering axioms, but also with their own styling concept that said function drives form, so that, for example, just about any shape was suitable for a fuel tank. But, beginning in the 1980s and reaching affirmation in the 1990s, we the people have turned the styling clock back to the triangular themes of the 1930s, 1940s, and 1950s. The "in" look of today draws directly from the Wigwam and from the old Harley factory in Milwaukee. "If eyes are made for seeing, then beauty is its own excuse for being," said Emerson. Indian motorcycles need no excuses.

As for the Indian saga, I think it's compelling for a number of reasons. Certainly the lost-cause element is powerful. If Indian riders participate in Civil War games, more than other groups they probably favor Confederate gray over Union blue. Beyond that, as with any old vehicle, there's a time-machine quality to Indians—more so than with old Harleys, I think, because the very name "Indian" on the tanks says these critters are from another world. Certainly all was not good in the good old days, but we like to pretend otherwise. When you straddle an Indian, crank it up, grab a handful, and pop the clutch, you're not just riding an old motorcycle, you're adding to the miles piled up by the legendary figures of the game. You're part of the club, along with Cannonball Baker and Iron Man Kretz.

There's a lot going on in today's antique-motorcycle movement. From the 1950s through the 1970s, the movement centered on static displays, or "shows" as we call them. In the 1980s organized antique-motorcycle-club rides of several days'

This Chief "rider" was restored in a popular configuration, combining the 1952–1953 front end and engine cowling with the 1940–1951 exhaust system. The "Scoot Boot" box on the luggage rack, a highly prized piece, was designed in the 1950s to fit on top of outboard motors. The bike is Indian dealer Bob Stark's personal mount. A champion "rider," this job has motored over 260,000 miles in the past 40 years!

Always popular during the production era were customs. These "bobbers" maintained stock frame and fork geometry and were the outgrowth of efforts to lighten and speed up the motorcycles. They're a different strain from the later "choppers," which were designed for a certain look regardless of functionality.

No need to leave Fido, uh, "Scout" at home. Jim and Debbie Christian, and Scout, enjoy the 1996 16th annual California Indian meet with their 1944 Chief and sidecar. Tim Cunningham

duration caught on. These are continuing to grow in popularity. Racing of antique motorcycles has become a valuable attraction for both racers and fans. Today, we see a matured movement, one in which with greater and greater frequency individual riders and small groups organize their own informal riding adventures on old motorcycles. The old-bike scene is healthy indeed when we straddle our 60-year-old motorcycles and chuff away on a 1,000-mile tour with all the nonchalance of the riders of the latest Harley, Honda, or you name it.

So hop on your Chief or other Indian today. Motor over to the Harley shop and pretend you

Owner/restorer Jim Dingess and wife Susan pack up for another day of adventure. The customized 1953 Chief had the 1990s Harley look. And what a place to have spent the night, just 30 feet from the rustling Colorado white waters shown in the next photo!

Indians are for riding, not just for collecting. "Motorcycling" is the game, not "motorcycles."

need some gunk. Watch the crowd gather around your oily old Indian, oblivious to the shiny new bikes. Conduct "the standard Indian briefing"—you know: (1) it's a 1947; (2) 1953 was the last year they were made; (3) no, parts aren't hard to get; and (4), yes, I did the work (or, no, the thus-and-so shop did the work). Chances are, you'll make another Indian convert somewhere within the crowd. Then, motor toward home, wave back at a waver, and return a thumbs-up to a thumbs-upper, just like you do every time you ride this old Springfield stallion. Think of that old sales slogan and how it's become a force in your life: "There's magic in the name Indian."

Appendix A

Colors and Other Finishing Details

Colors

1922–1923
Tank, fenders, chain guard, and frame, standard: Indian Red; optional, white or dark blue; double gold 3/64-inch stripes around tank edges; double gold 3/64-inch stripes around edges of front fender crown and double gold 3/64-inch stripes highlighting the valance; double gold 3/64-inch stripes around outside edges of rear fender. Horn, headlamp, and taillamp: black. Gearshift lever, kickstarter lever, compression-release hand lever on handlebar, luggage rack, and front-wheel bell cranks: bright nickel plating. *Sources: literature and recollections of former advertising department staffer Ted Hodgdon.*

1924–1929
Same as 1922–1923 except no documentation of optional colors for tank, fenders, and frame. *Source: sales literature.*

1930
Same as 1922–1923, with the added options of special Indian color combinations (unspecified) for the main areas and a different color within the tank panel bounded by the double gold 3/64-inch stripes. *Sources: period photos and sales literature.*

1931
Tanks, fenders, chain guard, and frame, standard: Indian Red lacquer (only year for lacquer instead of enamel); optional lacquer (only year) finishes of black with Japanese Red tank panel, Indian Red with cream tank panel, gray with green tank panel, dark blue with cream tank panel. Special colors (not specified) at extra cost. Some optional two-color finishes with double-line 1/64-inch gold striping on fenders to bound the contrasting color. *Source: Indian News.*

1932
Tanks, fenders, chain guard, and frame, standard no-extra-cost choices: Indian Red, black, Indian Dark (Police) Blue, and five other unspecified choices; gold pinstriping. *Source: Indian News.*

1933
Tanks, fenders, chain guard, and frame, standard no-extra-cost choices: Indian Red, black, dark blue, cream, Chinese Red, light blue, Indian Red with cream tank panel, black with Chinese Red tank panel, dark blue with light blue tank panel, light blue with Chinese Red tank panel, Chinese Red with black tank panel, light blue with dark blue tank panel, gold pinstriping in each case. Tanks, fenders, chain guard, and frame, optional extra-cost finishes: could be any colors available in DuPont DuLux enamel, plus special tank lettering, with gold pinstriping in each case. *Source: sales literature.*

1934
From sales brochure (Note: Brochure refers to "tank" instead of "tank panel" in each case, and period photos show some examples of tanks completely painted in one contrasting color.)

Tanks, fenders, chain guard, and frame, standard no-extra-cost color choices: Indian Red, black, dark blue, cream, Chinese Red, light blue, Indian Red with black tank, Indian Red with dark blue tank, Indian Red with cream tank, Indian Red with light blue tank, black with Indian Red tank, black with cream tank, black with Chinese Red tank, black with light blue tank, dark blue with Indian Red tank, dark blue with cream tank, dark blue with Chinese Red tank, dark blue with light blue tank, silver with any standard color tank, cream with light blue tank, Chinese Red with cream tank, Chinese Red with light blue tank, light blue with Indian Red tank, light blue with Chinese Red tank, gold pinstriping (gold Indian-head transfer on Sport Scout model only). Tanks, fenders, chain guard, and frame, optional extra-cost finishes: any colors available in DuPont Dulux enamel, plus optional color arrangements (gold Indian-head transfer on Sport Scout model only).

From 1934 Price List Indian Motocycles (dealer order blank)
Same as sales brochure with the following

exceptions/additions: contrasting tank finishes are referred to as "tank panel" instead of "tank," silver listed as an extra-cost color, special panels available at extra cost, and special striping at extra cost.

1935

Tanks, fenders, chain guard, and frame, standard no-extra-cost choices: Indian Red, black, dark blue, silver, Chinese Red, dark blue with light blue tank and fender panels, dark green with light green tank and fender panels, Indian Red with Chinese Red tank and fender panels, dark brown with cream brown tank and fender panels, black frame and fork with light blue main areas and yellow tank/fender panels, black frame and fork with dark blue main areas and silver tank/fender panels, black frame and fork with dark blue main areas and cream tank/fender panels, black frame and fork with Chinese Red main areas and silver tank/fender panels, gold pinstriping in each case, gold Indian-head transfer on all tanks. Optional tank panels: plain panel (outline of profile), Arrow panel (see illustrations), and V panel (see illustrations). *Source:* Indian News.

1936

Tanks, fenders, chain guard, and frame, standard no-extra-cost choices: Indian Red and a variety of other unspecified color combinations. Tanks, fenders, chain guard, and frame. Optional extra-cost choices: any special colors available in DuPont Dulux enamel. Tank trim as in 1935. *Source: sales Literature.*

1937

Tanks, fenders, chain guard, and frame, standard no-extra-cost choices: Indian Red. Tanks, fenders, chain guard, and frame, optional extra-cost choices: a new variety of other unspecified color combinations. Tanks, fenders, chain guard, and frame, optional extra-cost choices: any special colors available in DuPont Dulux enamel. Tank trim as in 1935 and 1936. *Source: sales literature.*

1938

Tanks, fenders, chain guard, and frame, standard no-extra-cost choices: maroon with orange tank and fender panels and green pinstriping (only instance of standard striping in other than gold), Indian Red, black with Chinese Red tank and fender panels, Mohawk Green with Seminole Cream tank and fender panels, Navajo Blue with Apache Grey tank and fender panels. Tanks,

fenders, chain guard, and frame, optional extra-cost choices: any special colors available in DuPont Dulux enamel. Tank trim: V or plain panels. *Source:* Contact Points.

1939

Tanks, fenders, chain guard, and frame, standard no-extra-cost choices: Indian Red, black, Metallic Cascade Blue, police (dark) blue, black with Chinese Red tank and fender panels, Metallic Cascade Blue with silver tank and fender panels, Metallic Santaupe (cross between beige and olive green) with Chinese Red tank and fender panels. Tanks, fenders, chain guard, and frame, optional extra-cost choices: any special colors available in DuPont Dulux enamel. Tank trim: World's Fair panel (see illustrations) or V (not documented but observed on unrestored 1939 Four of Max Bubeck). *Sources:* Indian News *and* Unrestored Motorcycle.

1940

All frames black, except where noted. Tanks, fenders, and chain guard, standard no-extra-cost choices: black (DuPont 93-005), Indian Red (DuPont 93-5388-R), Fallon Brown (DuPont 93-2174), Seafoam Blue (DuPont 93-1032), Kashan Green (DuPont 93-3888), and Jade Green (DuPont 93-502). *Sources: colors, by name,* The Motorcyclist; *color codes from a special Indian paint brochure (on file with Bob's Indian Sales).* Note: Sales literature mentions only black, red, and blue; period photos indicate light-colored Chiefs (white or Fallon Brown) with all surfaces in a light color except the center stand and side stand, and one example was described as white.

1941

All frames black, except where noted. Tanks, fenders, and chain guard, standard no-extra-cost choices: black (DuPont 93-005), "Brilliant" Red (may be advertising adjective or may mean a new shade, DuPont number unknown), Seafoam Blue (DuPont 93-1032), Brilliant Red with black fender skirts and chain guard, Seafoam Blue with black fender skirts and chain guard, white (DuPont number unknown) with black fender skirts and chain guard, white with Brilliant Red fender skirts and chain guard, white with Seafoam Blue fender skirts and chain guard. Note: Period photos indicate light-colored Chiefs (white or Fallon Brown) with all surfaces in a light color except the center stand and side stand, and one example was described as white.

1942

All frames black. Tanks, fenders, and chain guard, standard no-extra-cost choices: black (DuPont 93-005), "Brilliant" Red (may be advertising adjective or may mean a new shade, DuPont number unknown), Seafoam Blue (DuPont 93-1032). Tanks, fenders, chain guard, and frame, optional extra-cost choices: the same two-color schemes as on 1941 models cost $3 extra; special colors and combinations were available with prices individually provided upon application. *Source: 1942 Cash Delivered Price List of Indian Motorcycles, original copy on file with Chuck Myles Indian Agency.*

1943–45

All frames black. Tanks, fenders, and chain guard: blue, Navy (dark) Blue, or gray. *Sources: sales literature,* Indian News, *personal observations.*

1946

All frames black. Tanks, fenders, and chain guard, standard no-extra-cost choices: black, Red, Seafoam Blue, Police Silver. *Source: sales literature.*

1947

Same as 1946 except Police Silver not listed, plus some completely white (except black centerstand and sidestand) Chiefs by special order. *Sources: sales literature and* Indian News, *September–October 1947, page 10.*

1948

Same as 1946, plus Prairie Green. *Sources: sales literature and (for green)* Contact Points *No. 756, December 8, 1947.*

1949

No production.

1950

Same as 1946, except the Indian script on the tank had red paint along the inner surfaces of the letters (the "lowlights"). *Source: sales literature.*

1951

Same as 1950 except that some early-season Chiefs had the red Indian script "lowlights," but most Chiefs had black script "lowlights."

1952–1953

All frames black. Tanks, fenders, and chain guard: black (DuPont 0-94-70186–different from 1940 black), red (DuPont 0-94-658-M), medium blue (DuPont 0-94R-20953), yellow (DuPont 0-94-5348), green (DuPont 0-94-6282), light green (DuPont 0-94R-20952), Pimpernel Scarlet (DuPont 0-94-2622-R), cream (yellow) (DuPont 0-94-24988), Checker Flag Blue (metallic) (DuPont 0162-24989), Cocoa Brown (tan) (DuPont 094-55489), and olive drab (DuPont 094-20107). "Eighty" decal under Indian tank script. (DuPont numbers courtesy of Indian Motorcycle Supply Inc.)

Other Finishing Details

Bits and Pieces

1922–1929	some bright nickel-plated, some dull nickel-plated
1930–1938	some dull nickel-plated, some chrome-plated
1939–1953	some cadmium-plated, some chrome-plated

Crankcases and Transmission Cases

1922–1925	painted to match frame, tank, fenders, and chain guard
1926–1928	painted to match tank, fenders, and chain guard (optional) or unpainted
1929–1953	unpainted

Cylinders

1922–1931	dull nickel-plated
1932	some dull nickel-plated, some painted black
1933–1953	painted black

Exhaust Headers

1922–1936	dull nickel-plated
1937–1953	chrome-plated

Handlebars

1922–1946	black
1947	black; chrome at extra charge
1948–1953	chrome-plated

Mufflers

1922–1939	painted black
1940–1953	chrome-plated on new mach-ines, but in most years replacement mufflers were also offered with black paint

Spokes

1922–1930	black
1931–1953	cadmium-plated

Tires
1922–1924	natural rubber (art gum color) or white
1925–1953	black

Wheel Hubs
1922–1953	black

Wheel Rims
1922–1932	black
1933	black (standard) or cadmium-plated (optional)
1934–1946	black (standard) or chrome-plated (optional)

Motor and Serial (Frame) Numbers
1922–1930 Motor Numbers (No Frame Numbers)
1922	80T000-up
1923	Chief 61ci, 80V000-up
	Chief 74ci, 90V000-up
1924	Chief 61ci, 80X000-up
	Chief 74ci, 90X000-up
1925	Chief 61ci, 80Y000-up
	Chief 74ci, 90Y000-up
1926	Chief 61ci, AZ101-up
	Chief 74ci, AH101-up
1927	Chief 61ci, BZ101-up
	Chief 74ci, BH101-up
1928	Chief 61ci, CZ101-up (last year for 61ci)
	Chief 74ci, CH101 to CH2224
1929	Chief 74ci, CH2225-up
1930	Chief 74ci, EH101 to EH1535

1931–1953, motor numbers and frame numbers
Note: There were no motor and frame number indicators for special fast motors (such as B, Savannah, Daytona, and Bonneville).

1931	motor: EH1536 and up (conflicts with frame data)
	frame: H1410 and up (conflicts with motor data)
1932	motor: COC101-up
	frame: 303101-up
1933	motor: CCC101-up
	frame: 333101-up

1934	motor: CCD101-up
	frame: 334101-up
1935	motor: CCE101-up
	frame: 335101-up
1936	motor: CCF101-up
	frame: 336101-up
1937	motor: CCG101-up
	frame: 337101-up
1938	motor: CCH101-up
	frame: 338101-up
1939	motor: CCI101-up
	frame: 339101-up
1940	motor: CDO101-up
	frame: 340101-up
1941	motor: CDA101-up
	frame: 341101-up
1942	motor: some CDA numbers
	frame: some 341 numbers
	motor: CDB101-up
	frame: 342101-up
1943	no 1943-models
1944	motor: CDD101-up
	frame: 344101-up
1945	no 1945-models
1946	motor: CDF101-up
	frame: 346101-up
1947	motor: CDG101-up
	frame: 347101-up
1948	motor: CDH101-up
	frame: 348101-up
1949	no production
1950	motor: CEJ101-up
	frame: 3501001-up
1951	motor: C2001-up
	frame: C2001-up
1952	motor: CS6001-CS6500
	frame: CS6001-CS6500
	Note: some leftover 1952 models origanally registered as 1953 models
1953	motor: some four- and five-digit numbers near CS6501-CS61300
	frame: some four- and five-digit numbers near CS6501-CS61300
	Note: some numbers lower the 6501 were ariganally registered as 1953 models

Index

Accessory packages, 100, 101
Alzina, Hap, 40, 50
American Motorcycle Association (AMA), 49, 92
Arundel, Peter, 110
B motors, 21
Bennett, Wells, 62
British motorcycles, 116, 117
Brockhouse, 107, 112
Bubeck, Max, 78, 104–106
Burns, Albert "Shrimp," 18
Carter, Allen, 84, 92–95
Chase, Frank, 105
Christian, Frank, 76, 105
Clubs, 118–123
Clymer, Floyd, 52, 76
Cradle frame, 17
De Mark, Van, 50
Depression, 36
du Pont, E. Paul, 29, 39, 84
Elder, Sprouts, 40
Excelsior, 17
Free, Roland "Rollie," 55, 65, 67–70
Hallowell, Jimmy, 87
Ham, Fred, 60, 62
Harley-Davidson Motor Company, 12, 17, 18, 20, 23,
    26, 35, 41, 48, 49, 56, 57, 60, 88, 94, 114
Hedstrom, Oscar, 8, 10, 21
Hendee Manufacturing Company, 8, 10, 21
Hendee, George, 8, 10, 21
Henderson, 23
Highways, 34, 43
Indian Motorcycle Company, 21
Indian motorcycle models
    Ace, 23, 24, 27
    Big Chief, 20
    Bonneville Chief, 72, 75, 80, 82, 88, 98
    Chief, 14, 16, 18, 20, 22, 23–25, 27, 30–32, 34,
        36–41, 47–50, 54–58, 62–65, 67–72, 75, 76, 78,
        80–83, 86,–88, 90, 92–94, 96, 98–100, 102,
        104–106, 109, 110, 112–117
    Chout, 104–106
    Clubman, 101
    Daytona, 75
    Four, 27, 32, 62, 64, 71, 78, 92
    Junior Scout, 33, 64
    Prince, 22, 24, 26
    Roadmaster, 101
    Scout (new) 33, 34
    Scout 45 (Police Special), 23, 24
    Scout Pony, 32
    Scout, 12, 13, 16, 18, 20–23, 27, 32, 62
    Sport Scout, 47, 50, 54, 64, 69, 70, 72, 75, 92, 103
    Sportsman, 101
    Standard, 18, 21, 62
    Thirty-fifty, 33
    Traffic Car, 72, 74
Isle of Man Tourist Trophy (TT), 10
Johnson Motors, 76
Kretz, Ed, 68, 89
Laurer, Al, 50
Lisman, Bo, 50
Ludlow, Fred, 50, 69, 72
Mathewson, Harold, 40
Meador, Bill, 102
Motocycle, 8
Petrali, Joe, 60
Police motorcycles, 20, 23, 93, 112, 113
Powerplus, 11, 16, 18
Princess sidecar, 14
Racing, 83, 122
Reading-Standard, 16
Remally, Paul, 40
Ricardo heads, 48, 49
Robinson, Earl and Dorothy, 58
Rogers, Ralph B., 96, 102, 106, 110, 112
Russian project, 93
Scholfield, Kenny, 50
Seymour, Johnny, 60
Sidecars, 17, 101
Smith, L. C. "Smittie," 56–59
Touring, 43, 46, 47
TT events, 83, 87
Vehicle servicing, 43, 44
Vincent HRD, 106, 110
Vindian, 110
Weaver, Briggs, 102
Whiting, C. Randolph, 39, 40, 48, 50–53
Whiting, Roger, 48, 50
Wigwam, 12
World War I, 12
World War II, 88–95
World's Fair, 70